ABOUT LAW

An introduction

TONY HONORÉ

CLARENDON PRESS · OXFORD

Oxford University Press, Great Clarendon Street, Oxford OX2 6DP

Oxford New York
Athens Auckland Bangkok Bogota Bombay
Buenos Aires Calcutta Cape Town Dar es Salaam
Delhi Florence Hong Kong Istanbul Karachi
Kuala Lumpur Madras Madrid Melbourne
Mexico City Nairobi Paris Singapore
Taipei Tokyo Toronto

and associated companies in
Berlin Ibadan

Oxford is a trade mark of Oxford University Press

Published in the United States
by Oxford University Press Inc., New York

First published 1995
Paperback reprinted 1996, 2000

British Library Cataloguing in Publication Data
Data available

Library of Congress Cataloguing in Publication Data
Honoré, Tony.
About law: a short introduction/Tony Hororé.
p.   cm.
1. Law—Great Britain. 2. Law—Philosophy. I. Title.
KD662.H66 1995
349.41—dc20   95-23838   [344.1]
ISBN 0-19-876387-5
ISBN 0-19-876388-3 (pbk)

Printed in Great Britain
on acid-free paper by
Bookcraft (Bath) Ltd.
Midsomer Norton, Somerset

Contents

I
Law

Everyone knows something about law from personal experience, television or newspapers. This book is a brief introduction, with a minimum of technical terms, to the problems that law presents and to how lawyers go about solving them. It is meant for people who are thinking of studying law, or who are curious about it and would like to know more. Some of them may have heard that learning law is a matter of learning rules by rote. That is not true, and the reasons why it is not true are explained in the book.

The technical terms that cannot be avoided are explained as we go along and in a glossary at the end. I have tried to write simply, but do not pretend that the arguments are always straightforward. Law can be quite complex. That is part of its fascination.

THE AIMS OF LAW

Law has several aims. They are all concerned with making society more **stable** and enabling people to **flourish**. One way of doing this is to set up an **official framework of compulsion**. The law forbids certain ways of behaving, like murder, libel, and parking on double yellow lines, and requires others, like paying income tax. If people disobey the rules the law threatens them with something unpleasant (often called a sanction), like being punished or having to pay compensation. The idea is that within this framework of do's and don'ts people can live more securely. If they are more secure they will treat one another better.

A second aim is to **provide facilities** for people to make their own arrangements. Laws guarantee to people who buy and sell goods, make wills, take employment, form companies and so on that the state will if necessary enforce these arrangements.

A third aim is to settle **disputes** about what the law is and whether it has been broken.

Taking these three aims together, we see that law not only **threatens** those who do what it forbids but **promises** to protect people's interests. It imposes restrictions on them but also gives them certain guarantees.

Lastly, a very important aim of law is to **settle what the system of government is to be**. Today and for the last few hundred years we have been mainly governed by sovereign states. That is changing. We are now increasingly governed, indirectly or directly, by international bodies (for example through treaties such as those setting up the European Union). But the state still occupies centre stage, especially when it comes to enforcing laws.

These four aims are central to a system of law.

The state

The state has an important part to play in making and enforcing law. But what is a state? It is a political unit with a territory that the international community treats as independent, for example the United Kingdom, Barbados or Japan. Law settles how the state is to be governed (its constitution), what duties it owes its citizens, and what duties they owe to one another and to it. The law of the state consists, therefore, of a system of government, together with a framework for making the life of citizens more secure and for enabling them to flourish.

Since each state has its own **system of law**, there are many legal systems: the law of the United Kingdom, Barbados, Japan etc. The laws of states differ a bit but also have much in common. Legal systems are called systems because in each state or part of a state with its own laws there are official bodies concerned with the whole of its law. These bodies — the branches of the state — are the **legislature**, which makes laws, the **executive government**, which puts laws into effect, and the **judges**, who decide disputes about the law. These branches of government try to see that the laws do not conflict with one another. In other words, they treat the laws as parts of a system that hangs together.

International law

International law is an extra system on top of the state systems. It presupposes state law, and could not exist without it, because international law can only be enforced if states are prepared to put it into effect. But it serves a different community: the international community. International law is about the relations between independent states. It treats them as equals, whatever their population, wealth and power, so that in international law Barbados is on a level with Japan.

Like state law, international law consists of several elements. Again all of them aim at **stability** in international life and the **encouragement** of trade and other contacts between states. International law lays down how international bodies such as the United Nations are set up, and what powers they have (their constitution). It also says how states must treat one other, how they must behave to international bodies and how the international bodies must behave towards them. It provides facilities for states to make binding agreements (treaties) and for the settlement of disputes.

LAW, MORALITY AND SELF-INTEREST

Law cannot deal with the whole problem of how people, states and international bodies should behave to one another. Though the **threat of punishment** and other sanctions are often effective in the short run, in the long run law has to build on a basis of **morality and self-interest**. For instance, though fear of being caught out is an important motive for paying taxes, laws that impose taxes are in the long run effective only if most people think it right or in their own interest to make a contribution to the expenses of the state. If most people do think this, law can (within limits) settle what taxes there should be and how much each person should pay. It can impose penalties on those who do not pay their share. Of course not everyone will pay, but the majority probably will, and the minority, or many of them, will be caught and penalised.

Law builds on moral opinion and self-interest. But that is not the whole story. **Laws claim to be morally sound** — to be part of morality. They try to mould moral opinion. The existence of a law can convince people that what it requires is right and in people's interests. Tax law is a good example, because it is fair to make someone pay a tax only if other people in the same position are also forced to pay it. Indeed, even if people agree that they should make a contribution to the state's expenses, only a law can fix what that contribution should be. In this way **law and moral opinion support one another**. Morality is incomplete without law, and law can only be enforced when it is backed by morality and self-interest.

Here is a more dramatic example — a rule of international law that forbids aggression by one state against another. This rule is workable only if the governments of most states think it right and in their own interest to outlaw attacks of this sort. If they did not, it would be pointless to forbid state aggression. Indeed until this century many states, especially the powerful ones, did not think it in their interest to outlaw aggression. To build an empire by conquest was regarded as acceptable, and indeed in the best interests of the people conquered. So the ban on aggression has only recently come to be part of international law. Now, though some states still attack other states (e.g. Iraq attacked Kuwait), they do so more rarely. One reason for the change is that the rule of international law outlawing aggression has **strengthened the opinion that aggression is wrong and not in the best interests even of powerful states**.

Given a sufficient backing, then, from moral opinion and self-interest, a state can pick out some rules about behaviour and give them an official status as law. The international community can do the same. One advantage of turning rules about behaviour into laws is that the behaviour forbidden or demanded can be spelled out more exactly. The speed limit can be set at 70 miles an hour. Drivers then know that if they go faster than 70 they will be committing an offence and will be liable to a penalty. **Morality or self-interest on its own would not provide a clear guide** to the maximum speed.

Another advantage of making a rule of conduct law is that, if people or states do not conform, the law can **spell out the steps to be taken** against them. In this way the people or states concerned know pretty much what can happen if they step out of line. Offenders can be made liable to official measures of disapproval — sanctions. These range from the use of armed force and economic boycott to imprisonment, fines, disqualification and being made to pay compensation.

The limits of law

It does not follow that law should make compulsory every sort of behaviour that has the backing of morality and self-interest. For instance it is right to give presents on certain occasions, to return hospitality and to do favours for friends. These could be made into formal, legal duties; and in some societies they are. For instance in some places law fixes the amount of the gift that must be made to a bride's family on marriage.

There are arguments, however, for **not making everything that is morally right into a legal duty**. There is much to be said for keeping law to the minimum. To do this allows people more space to do what they like without interference. It is tempting to want to regulate every aspect of life, but to have too many laws irritates people and in the long run brings law into disrepute.

What is more laws, like other formal arrangements, are **expensive**, because the state has to find and pay for ways of enforcing them. If it allows many laws to become a dead letter, this undermines respect for the law in general. So the cost of imposing do's and don'ts by law often outweighs the likely benefit. Too much law creates a bonanza for lawyers without any real benefit to ordinary people.

LAWYERS

Law, then, consists of constitutional arrangements plus officially-backed rules that tell us how to behave or help us to make private arrangements or provide for settling disputes. These are all connected because the constitution settles who is entitled to lay down the rules.

In modern states three bodies play a part in settling what the law is. The **legislature** (in Britain, Parliament and the Queen) makes new laws and cancels or repeals old laws. The laws made by the legislature are **statutes**. The **executive** government (in Britain the Queen and her ministers) is given power by the legislature to make less important laws, like traffic **regulations**. **Judges** in deciding disputes interpret the laws and fill in the gaps in them. The law they make is **case-law**.

Lawyers study this triple system of official rules: statutes, regulations and case-law. Some lawyers advise legislators; some are judges; some teach law. But most advise private clients or organizations about the rules that apply to them in particular cases. If necessary, they argue their client's case in court.

To some people these activities have an endless fascination. Why? To be a good lawyer is more difficult than it seems. It is not just a matter of repeating rules to be found in statutes or regulations or case-law. Laws, however carefully drawn up, **do not solve all the problems that they are meant to solve**, or that in practice crop up.

Law

People and states lay down laws and make contracts and treaties and wills only to come up against a situation that they did not foresee. A man makes a will thinking that his children will outlive him. What happens if he outlives them? I agree to buy a house on the basis that I can sell my present house. Do I have to go on with the sale if I find that I cannot? Income is taxable, but do tips amount to income? Murder is forbidden, but is it murder to put a terminally ill patient who wants to die out of their misery? The answers are not obvious. Lawyers have to work them out.

So laws and arrangements that are legally binding (like contracts, wills and treaties) are permanently up for debate. How are they to be interpreted? Unsolved problems abound. But solutions cannot be plucked from the air. They must be reached in a way that **respects authority**. And in a legal system the authority comes from the constitution and attaches to the statutes, regulations and case-law that conform to the constitution.

To find the right (or best) solution to an unsolved problem calls for learning, wisdom, and restraint. **Learning**: the decision must be consistent with the history and traditions of a society and its laws. **Wisdom**: the solution must fit the facts of the case and the interests of the people concerned. **Restraint**: the law must build on what already exists. It must appeal to people's view of what is right and in their interest. It cannot leap too far ahead of opinion.

A lawyer is concerned, then, to find **the best solution to a conflict that is consistent with the authority of the constitution**. Lawyers can be just as grasping and unscrupulous as anyone else; but a good lawyer can hope in a modest way to make his community a better place. Brains are a help, but it is not necessary to be specially clever.

SECULAR LAW IN THE WESTERN TRADITION

This book is not specially about English or any other system of law. On the contrary, I have picked on problems to which the main Western legal traditions give different answers. Apart from the next chapter, on government, there will be little mention of whether this or that solution comes from England, France, Germany, the USA or elsewhere. But the book is confined to **secular law** in the Western tradition. It leaves out **religious systems of law**, like Islamic, Jewish, Hindu and Canon law, important though these are. Religious belief has deeply influenced Western law, but the law itself is not about religious beliefs and duties. It is about how society should be organized, and how people should treat one another whatever their beliefs.

Secular law takes the down-to-earth view that the concerns of this world can be treated on their own. As a separate branch of study it has its roots in the Roman republic and empire (Chapter 2). Nowadays most states all over the world have a system of law based on one of three models that have grown up over the last few hundred years: the **English**, the **French** and the **German**. In the rest of the world these have been followed, though not slavishly, and further developed.

English law and the systems based on it in the USA and other English-speaking countries are called **common law systems**. French and German law and the systems derived from them are the **civil law systems**. Though common law and civil law have grown closer, there are still notable differences between them. These, and the history that lies behind them, are explained in Chapter 2.

Despite these differences the law of a modern state has everywhere much the same shape and is concerned with the same problems. A legal system consists of:

(a) Constitutional or public law. This sets out the principles on which the society rests. It lays down how the power of the state is divided between legislators, government ministers, officials, judges and others. The constitution is often embodied in a written document, but in Britain it is largely unwritten. Constitutional or public law includes administrative law, which deals with the relations between officials and citizens and the ways in which people can object to official decisions, such as decisions about town planning.

(b) Criminal law. This defines as crimes or offences wrongs that the state thinks it should take steps to prevent, such as treason, murder, theft and driving without a licence. The state treats these offences as its own concern even when the victims are individuals, as they obviously are when someone is murdered or has his property stolen. Criminal law, which includes criminal procedure and punishment, lays down how these offences are to be investigated, prosecuted and tried, what sentences can be imposed on those found guilty, and how the sentences are to be carried out.

(c) Private law. This deals with the rights and duties of individuals towards one another, such as the duty to carry out a contract or to avoid injuring another person by your negligence. Here the state leaves it to the individual whose rights have been infringed to take action, and lays down the steps, such as claiming damages, that citizens can take to protect their interests. Private law includes what is called civil procedure. This is the procedure for bringing a lawsuit to make good your rights or claim compensation.

These divisions are not rigid, but they are worth bearing in mind.

As mentioned, this book does not try to set out the law of any particular country. There are good introductory texts for those who want to know the elements of the law of England. The same is true of many other countries. My book is more concerned with the problems law throws up than with the way in which this or that country tries to solve them. The problems we shall discuss are:

(1)   Does **history** explain the differences between the English common law and the civil law of most other countries?
(2)   Can and should law be used to **limit the power of governments**?
(3)   How and why do laws protect **property**?
(4)   What **agreements** do laws enforce and why?
(5)   What conduct does and should the state make **criminal**?
(6)   What conduct amounts or should amount to a **private wrong** (tort or delict)?
(7)   Are legal **procedures too formal**?
(8)   What is the best way to **interpret** texts?
(9)   What makes some laws **unjust**?

From dozens of topics that could have been chosen, I have picked nine of the most central. Obviously, they are treated only in outline. There is more to be said about all of them. I have gone for the broad sweep, and left out many exceptions and qualifications. Lawyers rightly insist on putting these in, and a complete account would include them. I have occasionally stated my own opinion; but for the most part the alternatives are set out, and readers left to judge for themselves.

There is no need to read this book through, or to read the chapters in any particular order. A reader who is bored by history (Chapter 2) or politics (Chapter 3) can go straight on to private law (Chapters 4,5,7) or criminal law (Chapter 6) as they feel inclined. The next three chapters, on forms, interpretation and justice, discuss some issues that crop up throughout the law. The book ends with a brief concluding chapter.

2

History

Why legal history is important

Some aspects of law cannot be understood except through its history. For instance, in the British constitution the House of Lords is part of the legislature. It is also the highest court of appeal. Why should this be?

No one devising a constitution today would choose to confer these powers on the House of Lords. In a democracy, legislators should represent the population as a whole. It should not, like the House of Lords, consist of aristocrats and people appointed for life by the government. Judges should not be part of the legislature. If they are, they are not truly independent.

The House of Lords has this strange combination of powers because **the modern House of Lords is the heir of the mediaeval magnates**. In the fourteenth century these magnates or peers obtained the right to be summoned to Parliament and to correct errors made by the ordinary courts of law. Their successors have kept these powers in a changed form, though they no longer reflect the balance of forces in Britain.

To explain the powers of the House of Lords historically is not to justify its place in the British constitution today. But the explanation helps to show how law evolves, or fails to evolve. A law for which there was originally a good reason can survive though that reason has vanished. Of course if laws are totally unsuited to new conditions they go under. In western countries the laws that treated women as inferior to men in voting, holding public office, making family decisions, owning property and earning money have over the last century almost vanished. The law has both reflected and helped to further this emancipation.

The House of Lords illustrates the other side of the coin. It does some useful work by amending badly thought-out bills, and has not thwarted the elected legislators in the House of Commons enough to make its abolition a priority. So up to now the House of Lords has survived. Its survival is an example of how laws (in this case a significant part of the constitution) can survive though they no longer serve their original purpose. The survival of laws has something in common with the survival of genes. The genes that allow us to walk upright survive, though so many people have back problems that we are clearly not well-suited to walking upright. But we are not so badly adapted to it that we have to crawl on all fours.

Unlike genes, laws are determined by our culture. We can change them. So why do ill-adapted laws often survive? One reason, apart from inertia, is that law aims to provide **security, psychological as well as physical**. One element in security is being able to know, and feel comfortable with, the formal rules that govern our society and our lives.

So continuity is important, and tells in favour of leaving laws as they are unless they prove utterly unworkable. It also explains why in all systems of law the previous decisions of courts are regularly followed when similar cases come up in the future. If it has once been decided that an elephant is a dangerous animal that decision is likely to be followed, though not all elephants are actually dangerous.

Precedents, as they are called, are important even when they are not formally binding. Not only ordinary people but judges, ministers and civil servants feel more at ease and less open to criticism if they follow past practice, unless there is a strong case for changing it. Justice also requires like cases to be treated alike. So it is not only the laws, but their interpretation, that tends to remain the same.

For historical reasons the laws of different countries can differ sharply. In particular there are differences between the civil law systems of continental Europe, South America and most of Asia and the common law systems of the English-speaking world. This chapter traces some of the factors that account for this.

Civil law and common law

One important theme is the relation between custom, writing and codes. In **civil law** systems the main branches of the law are embodied in **written codes**, which try to be comprehensive and clear. There are codes of criminal law, of criminal procedure, of private law, of commercial law, and perhaps others.

The codes are meant to contain the main principles of each branch of the law. Other statutes fill in the details. In fact the supplementary laws may be as important as the codes. For example in German tort law (see Chapter 7) the code imposes only liability for fault, but supplementary laws make railways etc. liable for accidents even if they were not at fault. All the same, the codes have a special prestige. They are not lightly altered.

Along with codes and supplementary statutes, scholarly writing, often by university professors, has an important place in civil law systems. Scholars explain and comment on the codes, statutes and decisions of courts. The views of the best of them are treated with respect. Court decisions are also important, but are anonymous. Individual judges remain in the background.

The same elements are to be found in **common law** systems, but in a different order of importance. Some common law systems have codes, but most do not. The statutes (apart from the constitution, if there is a written constitution) are all on a level. The decisions of judges of the higher courts are binding, and much of the law is left to the courts to develop. When a court consists of several judges, each can express a separate opinion. The opinions of individual judges have the sort of prestige that in civil law systems attaches to the opinions of scholars. Scholarly writing has some influence, and its influence is growing, but the opinion of practising lawyers — professional opinion — is more weighty.

In civil law systems, then, **reasoning from general principles** (to be found mainly in the codes or in scholarly writing) is the norm. Common lawyers argue more from case to case and tend to mistrust appeals to broad principle.

Suppose someone strikes my name off a database, so that I am not paid a pension to which I am really entitled. Has he committed a wrong against me? A civil lawyer would probably begin by asking whether I had suffered damage, whether the person who struck me off was at fault and whether his fault (if he was at fault) had caused the damage. A common lawyer would ask how like this is to other cases in which liability already exists. Is it like attacking my character ('defaming' me) by saying that I have pretended to pay the pension contributions that were due but have not really done so? Is it like making a false statement that harms me, by saying that I am not entitled to a pension when I am?

Though the contrast is not as sharp as it once was, civil and common lawyers still differ in the way they reason.

To understand why they do, we need to understand the importance of writing in legal development. Before writing comes to a society, its laws are customary. But customs without writing tend to be local and variable. Unless they are in the permanent form that writing gives them they seldom spread over a wide area or remain unchanged for long.

WRITTEN LAWS AND CODES

Written laws, cut in clay or stone, first appear in the middle east around 3000 BC. Rulers used them to advertise their success in war and devotion to justice. This would impress their subjects and spread a sense of security. Some of the earliest laws of which bits survive are the laws of Eshunna (about 1900 BC) and Hammurabi of Babylon (about 1750 BC).

Hammurabi's laws contain nearly three hundred sections. The king is the source of justice. Judges decide disputes, but with an appeal to the king. Though the laws refer to the favour of various gods, they are secular in character: they deal with such matters as contracts, crimes, property, marriage, divorce and trial procedure. Clearly Babylon was at this time already an organized state with a government.

Hammurabi's laws are generally called a code, but this term is misleading. His laws do not contain the whole law of Babylon. Rather they reduce some customs to a written form but leave others untouched. But when customs are put into writing, their character alters. They can no longer change gradually as they did before, because they are now set in a fixed form of words, a text. If there was previously a dispute about what the custom was, writing settles it.

For instance one of Hammurabi's laws lays down that if a son strikes his father, his hand is to be cut off. So, if there was previously a doubt about what the proper punishment was, this law settled it. But it also made the punishment difficult to change. Suppose it was later felt that to cut off the son's hand was too severe. In that case the text of the law stood in the way of reducing the penalty, say, to a fine.

There is some doubt whether Hammurabi **intended to change** the customary law. But there can be no doubt about the laws of **Solon**, the Greek statesman who in the sixth century BC was given the power to make laws for his strife-torn city of Athens. His laws cancelled debts for which the peasants had pledged their land or bodies. For the future he forbade loans on the security of a debtor's body, and so brought serfdom to an end. These were radical changes, and were seen as such.

Written laws, then, can serve as **propaganda** for a ruler, can tell subjects **where they stand** (provided they can read or can get someone to read for them) and can be used to introduce **reforms**. But even written laws, if they are to bind the ruler and so amount to more than propaganda, need an independent interpreter. How can a reliable and independent interpreter be found?

As soon as the law, written or unwritten, is at all complicated, there are people in every society who make it their business to become expert in it. In societies without a strong central authority wise men and women, who have a reputation for knowing the law, are consulted on difficult points. They are the first lawyers.

In a centralized state, where the ruler is powerful, it is not so easy to get independent advice about the law and see that it is followed. How can the ruler be prevented from twisting the law to suit himself? Physical force is usually on his side. What is needed is not the odd wise individual with a knowledge of the law, but a body of specialists who have some political clout.

ROMAN LAW AND LAWYERS

Rome was the first city and state where specialists of this sort emerged. Like the Athenians in the time of Solon, the Romans made an early collection of laws, the **Twelve Tables**, about 450 BC. They treated this as the source of their law and saw it, in retrospect, as part of a political revolution. This revolution abolished the monarchy and substituted a republic, in which the rulers were elected and held office only for a short time.

The specialists who interpreted the Twelve Tables and the unwritten part of the law were called **pontiffs**. At first they dealt with both sacred law (how to appease the gods) and secular law (how to secure peace among men). Some of them later confined themselves to secular law. As an example of how they interpreted the law, the Twelve Tables said that if a father sells his son three times (into bondage, to pay off debts) the son is to be free from his father's power. The Twelve Tables said nothing about a daughter. The pontiffs held that if a father sold his daughter once, she was free.

In the course of time the pontiffs lost their monopoly of interpretation and **secular lawyers extended their activities**. They gave opinions to people who consulted them, helped them to draft documents, advised them on the proper way to litigate, and taught students both privately and in public. They advised the magistrates and, when Rome became an empire, the emperor. Some argued cases in court and wrote books about the law. In fact they did nearly everything that lawyers do nowadays. The advice they gave was regarded as a form of unwritten law (even if the advice was in writing). This was because it was not the words they used, but the idea behind them, that bound the judge to whom the advice was given.

Many Roman lawyers (often called jurists) had political clout because they came from leading families. Those who did not used their legal expertise as a stepping stone to high office. They were a small, elite group of intellectuals, the first to make law a strict discipline. Unpaid in the republic, many held paid offices in the Roman empire. But the tradition of independence that had been built up earlier was not lost. Their outlook was progressive. As one of them, Pomponius, remarked, there can be no law without lawyers to improve it day by day.

Lawyers as advisers, not judges

It may seem strange that in the Roman world, which valued law highly, legal experts were advisers rather than judges. But so long as a society thinks that the ruler should do justice personally, the legal input has to come from elsewhere. If the laws are at all intricate, the ruler will not be expert in them. The role of lawyers is then to advise the ruler about the law rather than to sit in judgment themselves.

The idea that the ruler should not himself be a judge, and should not interfere with judges, comes much later. It was not until 1607 that James I of England was told by Chief Justice Coke that he was not learned in the law and so could not judge a lawsuit himself. The king strongly disagreed, but his view was rejected.

In the next century (1748) the French writer Montesquieu argued that, for citizens to be truly free, the main powers of government must be in the hands of different people. So the legislative power of making laws, the executive power of carrying them out and the judicial power of judging whether they had been broken should be separate. This theory (the **separation of powers**: see Chapter 3) dominated the American constitution of 1787 and is now widely accepted. Where it is taken seriously judges cannot be dismissed for giving decisions that the government dislikes, but only for corruption or incompetence.

In the Roman empire there was no separation of powers and no political freedom. All power lay with the emperor. But there can be **civic freedom without political freedom**. People can have private rights though they lack political rights. The idea that citizens had rights took root in Rome. They had the right to own and dispose of property, to preserve their family status and citizenship, to have their contracts enforced, and to have their tax liability settled by law. Though the emperor and the untrained judges he appointed decided lawsuits, judges were expected to follow the advice of expert lawyers about what the law was.

Over the period between 100 BC to 300 AD Roman lawyers published hundreds of law books aimed at judges and students. There were commentaries on statutes and books on special topics like mortgages and adultery. Lawyers' opinions to clients or magistrates who consulted them were collected and published. There were also teaching manuals. The writings of the leading lawyers came to be thought of no longer as advice that was binding on magistrates (unwritten law), but as a form of written law, a set of texts to be interpreted, along with the statutes enacted by the emperor.

But this material was too vast to be manageable. Between 529 and 534 AD the eastern emperor **Justinian** reduced it to three volumes, which still came to about a million words in all. The three volumes together made up the 'civil law'. Justinian's law books (his codification, as it is called) were different from the laws of Hammurabi, Solon or the Twelve Tables, and not merely in length. He wanted them to be complete and consistent. There was to be no law except what was in them. The laws were to stand on their own feet, with no need for interpretation (see Chapter 9).

But laws never cover every case that may arise, since we never foresee the future correctly. Writing always needs to be interpreted and added to. Besides, Justinian's law books were too bulky to be a code in the modern sense — a short statement of all the main principles of the law, or a branch of it. They were more like an unwieldy collection of cases and commentaries on the law, admittedly of high quality. But their flaws, and the fact that the books went into so much detail, turned out to be a blessing in disguise.

CIVIL LAW IN WESTERN EUROPE

The western Roman empire collapsed in the fifth and sixth centuries AD. Six hundred years later the scholarly study of law revived, starting in Bologna, the first university in Western Europe, around 1088 AD. Despite the gap in time, Charlemagne (768-814) and his successors, the 'Holy Roman Emperors of the German nation', had been treated in the west as Justinian's heirs. So Justinian's laws were still the laws of Western Europe. The universities therefore taught law students Justinian's civil law, as opposed to the customary law of Saxony, Burgundy, Castile, England and so on.

Between 1100 and 1500 universities spread all over Europe, from Sicily to Scotland and Portugal to Poland. The law syllabus was everywhere the same: Justinian's civil law. At the same time lawyers of the Western church began to collect and study church laws, or canons. The most important collection of these dates from about 1140. **Canon law**, as church law was called, was studied in the universities alongside civil law. Since the Western church had jurisdiction over marriage, wills and lawsuits between clerics, canon law was a separate system. Civil and canon law, however, both being basically Roman, had much in common. Each influenced the other.

At first civil lawyers studied the texts in Justinian's codes one by one. Then they began to search for the general principles to be found in them, and tried to fit the customary laws of the states where they were living into the civil law. The drawbacks of Justinian's law books now proved to be merits. They were a treasure house in which the lawyer or administrator could almost always, if he looked hard enough, find ideas and solutions adapted to the changed conditions of the later Middle Ages and Renaissance. The contradictions they contained were a help. They gave the civil lawyer a choice between different rules.

In the states into which Europe came to be divided **university-trained lawyers were made judges and advisers**. These lawyers naturally applied civil law whenever local customs did not settle the dispute. Around 1400 it came to be accepted that this was the right thing to do. Except when the church had jurisdiction, for example over wills, civil law governed the affairs of lay people wherever custom was silent. And civil law meant Justinian's law as understood after some three centuries of study in the universities.

The process by which civil law became the subsidiary law of most of Europe is called the **reception of Roman law**. England, we shall see, was an exception. There, Roman law had some influence but was never received wholesale.

The civil law was supposed to be uniquely rational. It was described as **written reason**. But from the sixteenth century onwards it was sharply attacked. The Renaissance unleashed a critical spirit that had previously been dormant. The reformation undermined the Western church. The emergent nation states rejected the Holy Roman (really German) empire. Each state claimed to be **sovereign** and to decide for itself what its laws should be. Church courts lost much of their jurisdiction. The civil law now seemed riddled with irrational and obsolete rules.

But a system of written law can only be replaced by other written laws. One cannot revive vanished customs by abolishing written laws. In the eighteenth century critics of the civil law therefore started a movement to replace Justinian's books by new codes of law. The new codes were to be drastically shorter than Justinian's books. They were to be well arranged and easy to understand. Each state was to have its own code.

Modern codes

The new codes were in practice drafted by lawyers with a university training. The earliest efforts read rather like textbooks. But towards the end of the eighteenth century better codes began to emerge. They tried to do two things. One was to provide an **answer to every question** that might come up, and so reduce the judge's discretion to a minimum. It was thought that judges, trained in the civil law, would otherwise obstruct change. The other aim was to provide a **handbook** that every citizen, if literate, could understand. The law should not be shrouded in mystery.

The code that came nearest to meeting the first aim was the **Prussian code of 1794**. It ran to 17,000 sections. Its author, Suarez, put the question 'Can written laws be short?'. He answered it by saying that we really need two sorts of law alongside one another. The one should be detailed and addressed to the judge, the other short and addressed to the citizen.

But this idea is impracticable. The short and the long version are bound sometimes to conflict. Which is then to prevail? If the long version prevails, the citizen's handbook is seen as just that: a useful explanation of the law but not a text that will bind judges when they come to decide cases.

Nevertheless the ideal of a code that the citizen can understand is appealing. Whereas Justinian's law books were clearly addressed to an elite, modern codes, with the spread of literacy, are partly meant to tell citizens what they must do to comply with the law. **Napoleon's code of 1804**, dealing with private law, came closest to realising this dream. It had only 2,283 sections and spread by conquest and imitation over much of western and southern Europe and South America.

But if a code is short and simple much depends on the interpretation that courts put on it. By the time the French code reached its centenary in 1904 it was obvious that it had to be interpreted in a way that took account of the social and economic changes of the nineteenth century. Much of the law was to be found not in the words of the code but in their interpretation by the courts and in supplementary statutes.

In an industrial age law is anyhow so complex that the 'citizen's handbook' ideal goes overboard. The text of a statute, for example a tax statute, cannot be understood by an ordinary citizen without an expert to explain it. That is no reason for drafting laws in obscure language, but it means that no one can put in his pocket a slim volume setting out the laws of his country, to be consulted when need arises.

It is no surprise, then, that the first important code of the industrial age, the **German code that came into force in 1900**, made no concessions to the layman. It was and is a masterpiece of technical legal design, the parts of which fit together in an intricate pattern. In theory an expert should be able by studying it carefully to find the answer to almost any problem that comes up. But experience has shown that even it needs to be supplemented by scholarly writing and court decisions if it is to fit modern life.

THE ENGLISH COMMON LAW

No written laws, and no system of codes, can answer all the problems that life presents. So **are codes really necessary?** Would a system of law be more responsive to social needs without them? This brings us to the common law of English-speaking countries, which developed for many centuries without codes and without university-trained lawyers. Indeed even today common law systems rely much less on codes and on theory than do civil law systems.

In England as in the rest of Europe the mediaeval universities, Oxford and Cambridge, studied civil and canon law rather than the local law. But, in contrast with most of Europe, university graduates did not shape the law of England. The common law of England was (and largely still is) an **unwritten law**. It was created in the Middle Ages by the royal courts and the advocates who argued cases in these courts.

This unwritten law was based on **professional tradition** and, later, the **opinions of judges** in deciding cases. The sense in which it is unwritten is that, even if judges give opinions in writing, as they now do, it is not the precise words they use but the idea that lies behind the words that counts as law. There was also (and is) written law in the form of statutes. But most of the common law developed quite independently of statutes. The common law does not consist of texts.

Common law originally meant the common law of England as opposed to local laws of, say, Wessex or Mercia. England acquired a common law at an early date because it had a strong centralized monarchy before most other parts of Europe. In the twelfth century, under Henry II (1154–1189 AD), the **royal courts extended their jurisdiction** at the expense of local and feudal courts. In deciding cases they created and applied the 'law and custom of the realm', which was distinct from both civil and canon law. Indeed by the time that civil law was received in other countries (from about 1400 onwards) the common law was too well established to be displaced.

In England litigation had to be begun by an order, called a **writ**, issued on the king's authority. There were different writs for different claims, such as the writ of right, to recover land; the writ of debt, to recover money owing; and the writ of trespass, to complain of a breach of the peace, such as a beating-up. The common law developed through argument by lawyers, including judges, about these writs. When were they available and what remedies did they give? As a result, the common law, unlike the civil law, is in many ways a law of remedies.

For example, rulers and magnates everywhere find it convenient to imprison their enemies without trial. England developed a remedy against this abuse, the writ of **habeas corpus**, which means 'you are to produce (in court) the body (of the person detained)'. Once the person was produced in court the judge could order him to be freed if there was no legal justification for detaining him. This remedy played a prominent part in the political struggles between king and Parliament in the seventeenth century — a century before the theory was accepted in civil law countries that personal freedom rules out imprisonment without trial.

Equally important in the development of the common law was the fact that both criminal and most civil lawsuits came from the thirteenth century onwards to be **tried by jury**. It was understood that the jury should decide what the facts of the case were. The judges and advocates had to work out what the law was so that the issues of fact could be put to the jury. This separation of fact and law never became part of civil law systems. It accounts for the fact that the common law is a more oral system of law, grounded in argument face-to-face, than the civil law, in which writing played and still plays a dominant part.

The common law was therefore built up by judges and advocates. They soon became a closely-knit profession. By about 1300 it was accepted that, though the king appointed judges, he could only choose them from among senior advocates, whose profession was to argue cases before the king's courts. These advocates, called by different names at different times (serjeants-at-law, barristers) formed with the judges an elite group of learned lawyers, like the Roman jurists. The Roman jurists had also built up their law by arguing about remedies. But in the hands of the university-trained lawyers of mediaeval and modern Europe the civil law became a system centred on principles and rights rather than remedies.

Legal education in the common law took place on the job. Students listened to cases being argued and practised arguing about cases, real and imaginary, among themselves. University education in the common law came on the scene much later. It was not until 1839 that the University of London gave the first academic degree in English law. The first American chair of law was created in 1799 and by 1850 there were fifteen law schools in different parts of the USA.

Civil and common law come closer

In the last 150 years university-trained lawyers have gained influence in the common law. They have made it more rational and less piecemeal. Case-law made by judges has become more important in the civil law. The civil and common law systems have thus come closer together. But they bear the marks of their origins. Civil law is the creation of two elites, a Roman elite of specialist legal advisers and an European elite of university-trained lawyers. The common law is the creation of an English (and more recently English-speaking) elite of judges and senior advocates. These origins explain the differences of style and method of reasoning that still separate the systems. In the history of law, as in history generally, the distant past is often the key to the present.

3
Government

Some governments are dictatorships of a person or party; others are constitutional governments. Constitutional governments are not all democratic, but in all of them there are **some legal limits on the power of the rulers**. In practice these limits can only be imposed by law, backed by public opinion. Indeed one of the main, and one of the oldest, functions of law is to limit the power of governments. Democracy makes the restrictions more effective, because in a democracy the rulers know that they will have to stand for re-election.

It is true that, apart from legal limits on its powers, there are **practical limits** to what a government can do by way of oppressing its subjects. Some are technical. It is not easy even with modern devices to spy on people at home. Morality and self-interest also play a part: the scruples or calculations of rulers or those to whom they give orders. The rulers may feel that there are things, like imprisoning the opposition without trial, that they should not do even when they would find it convenient. Or the army and police may be reluctant to arrest and shoot the government's opponents.

But only law can give the limits on government power a settled form. A **law that forbids imprisonment without trial** for more than so many days is quite likely to be respected. It can be relied on with some confidence by the person arrested, his family and advisers. A **feeling that it is morally wrong or politically dangerous** to imprison an opponent without trial is much less reliable. How wrong or dangerous the rulers think it to be will vary from case to case. The disappearance of an opposition leader will be noticed. If a teenager from an obscure family vanishes, his fate will hardly stir the waters. If the teenager belongs to a subversive group, the case against killing him will seem to the rulers a weak one. They might as well have him arrested and shot.

Morality and self-interest, then, are not enough by themselves to ensure that rulers behave decently. But they are the foundation on which legal restraints on government have to build, because laws

limiting their power will not be effective unless the rulers themselves
accept them.

THE RULE OF LAW

Most citizens, and nearly all lawyers, think that governments should
be subject to the 'rule of law'. But what is the rule of law? It exists
when a **government's powers are limited by law and citizens have
a core of rights** that the rulers are bound to uphold, and actually do
uphold.

A society may observe its own laws without observing the rule of
law. Suppose it has a law that citizens can be detained indefinitely
without trial. In that case, if a citizen is arrested and detained without
trial, the laws of that society are respected, but the **rule of law is
violated**. This is because, if citizens can be kept in prison for the rest
of their life without being tried, any other rights they may in theory
have are almost worthless. For the rule of law to prevail some laws,
like the detention without trial law, are ruled out.

The rule of law is an attractive ideal. But to impose limits on
government power is **expensive**. If the limits are to be effective,
there must be independent bodies (generally courts) to see that they
are respected. If the powers of government are curbed, it **takes longer
to reach decisions**. Government becomes more complicated, and in
an extreme case can grind to a halt. A poor country cannot afford all
the limits on government that may be possible in a richer one.

The advantages of the rule of law are obvious, so long as it is not
too expensive and does not paralyse government. But how far should
the restraints on government go? Opinions differ. The **trustful school
of thought** holds that the legal limits on government should be kept to
a minimum. They favour strong, decisive government. This outlook
has traditionally been dominant in Britain, though opinion is now
changing.

The **sceptical school of thought** reckons that governments are not
to be trusted. It sets out to multiply legal controls over them. These
controls may take various forms: the separation of powers, federalism,
bills of rights, judicial review (these will be explained). The sceptical
view prevails in the USA, where all these controls exist. Most other
countries fall somewhere between the two.

We shall be weighing up the argument between the trustful and sceptical views. I take the British constitution as an example of the trustful and the American constitution as an example of the sceptical view. It is worth noting that the British constitution is largely unwritten while the American constitution is mainly to be found in a written document, the Constitution, that first came into force in 1789, though it has been amended since. The sceptical school mistrusts any undertaking that is not in writing.

The trustful school thinks that the limits on government power should be few. In a country like Britain a good way of making sure that the limits are few is to have a **sovereign legislature**. This is because in Britain the government has to resign if it loses the support of the legislature (the House of Commons in particular). So the government normally has to have and does in fact have the support of the legislature; and it can exercise any powers that it can persuade the legislature to give it.

Sovereignty

The British Parliament, consisting of the House of Commons, the House of Lords and the Queen, is an example of a sovereign legislature.

Sovereignty is a slippery idea. It can be external or internal or both. **External sovereignty** is independence in international law. A state that is recognized as independent is a sovereign member of the international community. Of course states, even the most powerful, are not free to do exactly as they choose. They lack the resources to do some things, and international law prevents them from doing others. For instance, a state is **not allowed to use force** against another state **except in self-defence** or with the authority of the Security Council of the United Nations.

Another limit on a state's freedom of action is that it is legally **bound by the treaties** it makes. For example the members of the European Union have a treaty with one another by which much of their economic life is governed by the Union. The **European Union** has it own system of law and its own court, the European Court of Justice. The European Court of Justice takes the view that, if the law of the Union conflicts with the law of a member state, such as Italy or Britain, the law of the Union prevails.

Despite this, the **members of the European Union remain sovereign states**. It is merely that they have handed over a great deal of power to bodies like the Brussels Commission and the Council of Ministers, on which they are represented. A private citizen can do the same. To get rich quick I can agree to work for a bullying tycoon who insists on impossible hours and ruins my private life. This temporarily limits my freedom (which is for me what sovereignty is to the state) but does not destroy it. I can, if I want, leave the tycoon's service — and no doubt pay a price.

In much the same way the states that are members of the European Union **could leave it**. This would be against the law of the Union, and sanctions might be imposed on them by the other states, but it could be done. The other states could not use force against the state that seceded. They would not have the right to do what the northern states of the USA did when the southern states seceded from the American Union in 1861. They could not use force to keep the seceding state in the European Union. The reason is that the states that belong to the European Union, like Britain, are independent states, internationally recognized. The states of the USA, like Virginia, though they claimed the right to secede, are not independent states in international law.

A sovereign state, though legally independent, may in practice be influenced or even dominated by another state. The government of Lesotho, which is entirely surrounded by South Africa, is forced to pay close attention to the views of the South African government, whether it likes them or not. But it is **not legally bound** to do what the South African government tells it to. It can and does negotiate treaties with South Africa, for instance about its water resources.

The external sovereignty of a state is its independence in international law.

THE TRUSTFUL VIEW: LEGISLATIVE SOVEREIGNTY

Internal sovereignty, on the other hand, consists in the right of the legislature of a state to make any law it pleases. Internal sovereignty is legislative sovereignty. In a country like Britain the sovereign legislature (the two Houses of Parliament plus the Queen) could make a law, for example, abolishing elections. It could even lay down that people who criticized the law abolishing elections should be detained without trial. That law would be an outrage, but it would be valid in Britain. British courts would have to apply it. Of course a conscientious judge might refuse to do so and resign.

Despite this, supporters of legislative sovereignty argue that in democratic countries the legislature can be relied on not to pass a law of this sort. If it did, there would be violent protests and perhaps revolution. And it is, they think, valuable for the legislature to have unlimited legal power. In time of crisis, such as war, it would be wise to pass a law postponing elections until the crisis was over, and to have people who were suspected of working for the enemy detained without trial (this happened in Britain in the war of 1939–45). If the law forbade the legislature to make laws of this sort, the country would be hamstrung in conducting the war, and might lose it.

Even if this argument is convincing, the idea of legislative sovereignty is not as simple as it looks at first sight. If the legislature consists of a single person, a dictator, the only question is whether, to be laws, his wishes must be expressed in a certain form, such as writing.

But if the legislature **consists of two or more people or bodies** an awkward problem arises. In many countries laws are made by a lower house (like the House of Commons), an upper house (like the House of Lords) and a head of state (the monarch or president). To make a law all three must agree on the same written text. But how do they have to agree? In what order? By what majority? What happens if they disagree?

It is not obvious how to answer these questions. There are two basic possibilities. One is that laws must provide the answer. The other is that the matter is to be settled by custom. Customs of this sort, which regulate the way in which government works, are called **conventions**. A convention is a **practice that people in political life think they are bound to respect though it is not laid down in any law**. The questions we have put can be settled either by convention or law or a mixture of the two.

In answering them the trustful school favours convention and the sceptical school law. Convention grows up more easily when, as in Britain, there has been a long period of development unbroken by revolution or foreign conquest. A supporter of convention will argue that each House of the legislature should decide for itself what procedure to follow when it considers whether to agree to a proposed law. It should decide how many times the proposal needs to be approved (how many 'readings' there should be) and what majority in favour is needed if it is to pass. If the parts of the legislature disagree the trustful school would leave it to the good sense of each to decide whether to give way.

A good example of this approach is the convention in Britain that the **Queen should agree to a proposed law** if both Houses of Parliament have already agreed to it. This reflects the idea that Britain is a constitutional monarchy in which the Queen represents the people but does not personally exercise power. But then why should the monarch, if she has no political power, be part of the legislature? One explanation is that this makes for continuity (see Chapter 2).

A supporter of the convention about the Queen can also argue that it is a good thing to keep the head of state as part of the legislature because this helps to prevent laws being passed that violate the rule of law. It may be important for the members of Parliament to bear in mind that the head of state **could legally refuse to agree** to an outrageous law, like the one abolishing elections. The fact that there is a convention that she should agree, rather than a law by-passing the need for her to agree, helps to prevent an abuse by the legislature of its powers.

The other side of the coin is shown by the disagreements that took place in Britain early this century (1909–11) between the House of Commons and the House of Lords about whether the House of Lords had the **power to reject a budget** passed by the House of Commons. Here the problem **could not be solved by convention**, because the House of Lords did not admit that it ought, in a democratic society, to give way to the view of the House of Commons. Hence laws were passed in 1911 and again in 1949 to reduce the power of the Lords, so that it can only delay legislation for a shortish period. The House of Lords had of course to agree to these laws, which it did, under the threat that the existing members would be swamped by hundreds of new members who favoured the change.

Though conventions have the advantage of being flexible, so that they can change as conditions alter, this example shows that they are not viable when those who have to work them are pig-headed. So is it better to regulate the procedure for legislating by law than by convention?

It often is. Suppose that in a country like Britain with a sovereign legislature the opinion gained ground that **there should be a refer-endum** of all electors before any law was passed changing the constitution. If this was done by convention there would be a temptation for the government, if it did not want to hold a referendum that it might lose, to pretend that the proposed law did not change the constitution. So, if the referendum idea is to be taken seriously, it would be better to make the change by law. If that is done the courts (or some other independent body) will decide whether the proposed law alters the constitution, and so whether a referendum is needed.

But there is another snag. If a sovereign legislature passed a referendum law of this sort, could it not repeal it later by passing another law, without holding a referendum on the repealing law?

It is not easy to say. Some think that a sovereign legislature can repeal any law it has made previously. But would this be true even if the referendum law laid down that it (the referendum law) could not be repealed without a referendum?

Others think that the old legislature (in Britain Parliament and the Queen) **could not repeal the referendum law**, because that law would have changed the body that makes laws about the constitution. The referendum law makes the electors part of the law-making body whenever the constitution is to be changed. If the old legislature tried to change the constitution without a referendum they would not be making a law at all. The supposed law would be so much waste paper.

THE SCEPTICAL VIEW: CHECKS AND BALANCES

In a cohesive society, whose members share a common moral and political outlook, there is much to be said for the trustful view of government. There is also something to be said for it in a poor society, because it is expensive to impose limits on state power. Limited government calls for able, independent people, generally judges, to monitor the limits imposed. In a poor society there may not be enough of these to go round.

But if the society is **fairly wealthy and is divided into rival groups**, ethnic, religious, or social, law can be used to see that the interests of each person and group are taken into account when laws are made. If there are disputes about the laws or the way in which they are applied the state can arrange for independent people (normally judges) to decide whether the laws agree with the constitution and whether they have been properly applied by the government. In that case government has to be limited by law. Checks and balances are called for.

If there are to be effective checks and balances a written constitution is essential. Clearly conventions will not work, because the rival groups do not trust one another enough. A written constitution, like that of the USA, is needed if checks and balances are to work.

What sort of checks and balances are wanted? The most important are those that divide up state power. The **separation of powers** divides state power according to function. **Federalism** divides it according to geographical region. **Bills of rights** divide power between the state and ordinary citizens.

The separation of powers

The state has three main functions: legislative, executive and judicial. The **legislature** makes laws; the **executive** enforces the laws and governs the country; the **judges** decide disputes that come before them and in doing so interpret the law and apply it to the facts of the case they have to judge.

Two ideas underlie the separation of powers. The first is that, to avoid **too much concentration of power**, the same people should not legislate, govern and judge. Each branch of the state should be **independent** of the others. But if each branch is independent of the others, the danger is that they will each go their own way and abuse their powers. Each will be selfish and corrupt. To avoid this, a second idea comes into play. There should be some way in which **each branch can be kept in check by the others**.

The American constitution adopts both these ideas. The three branches of the state are separate. The legislature is the Congress, consisting of an upper house (Senate) and a lower house (House of Representatives). Executive power is in the hands of the President, who heads the government. Judicial power is in the Supreme Court. No one can be both a legislator and a member of the government, or a legislator and a judge, or a member of the government and a judge.

The three branches are separate in that no one can belong to two of them at a time. But each can be checked by the others if it abuses its powers. The President can veto legislation passed by Congress, though the Congress can then overrule him by a two-thirds majority. The President and judges of the Supreme Court can be charged by the Senate with various crimes (impeached) and if necessary removed from office. The judges of the Supreme Court are chosen by the President but have to be confirmed by the Senate. To make sure that the legislature keeps within its powers the Supreme Court has decided that, if the point comes up in a case before it, it can decide whether a law passed by Congress is against the constitution. If it is, the Court can say so, and the supposed law is then not a valid law. The President and Congress have accepted that the Supreme Court possesses this power.

In contrast the **legislature and executive in Britain are not separate**. The executive government (cabinet and ministers), who govern the country and execute the laws, belong to the legislature. The government depends on the legislature, since by convention it must resign if it loses the confidence of the House of Commons. But the House of Commons also depends on the government, because if the government decides that the time has come to call a general election the members of the House will (almost certainly) have to face re-election and may lose their seats.

The judges in Britain are more independent, since a judge of the higher courts cannot be dismissed except when the legislature asks the Queen to dismiss him for misbehaviour. Even so, the highest judges are members of the House of Lords, which is part of the legislature. And their independence is less important than it is in the USA, since they cannot declare that a law made by the legislature is against the constitution and so invalid.

Federalism

State power can also be divided up on a **geographical basis**. The system for doing this is called federalism. In a federal state there is a **federal government**, legislature and courts. There are also **regional governments**, legislatures and courts. Both may get their powers from a **written constitution**. Powers to make laws, to govern and to judge are each divided between the federal state and the regions. The regions go by different names in different countries (states, provinces, lands, cantons, republics).

One reason for dividing power in this way is that the country is **too large** to be governed conveniently from a single centre (Australia, the USA). Another is that its **regions vary** in language or culture (Switzerland, India, Canada). A third is that a **central government**

might be too powerful if it was not balanced by regional governments with some independent powers (Germany, the USA).

In a typical federation defence and foreign policy belong to the federal government, education to the regions, and the power to tax is divided between the two. So the federation and the regions may both have power to make laws on similar subjects. Since each region has its own independent powers and courts, it has its own regional legal system, alongside the federal legal system.

This makes for complication in a country like the USA where there are fifty 'states' (i.e. regions) as well as the federation itself. There are bound to be demarcation disputes between the federation and the regions, which have to be settled by courts, normally the federal courts. So lawyers flourish. If the federation also separates the law-making, governing and judging functions the law becomes very complicated and expensive. But the **complication and expense may be worthwhile** if they allow a country to hold together when otherwise it would fall apart.

Bills of rights

Another way of dividing up powers is to divide them between the state and private citizens. This is done by **listing in a law certain basic rights of citizens**. If there is a written constitution the list will be part of the constitution. When a bill of rights is in force a citizen has some rights that **cannot be taken away** from him either by the legislature, or the government, or the courts. (Whether the bill of rights itself can be repealed depends on the constitution).

For instance, if a citizen has the right not to be imprisoned for more than so many days without trial the legislature cannot make a law that provides for imprisonment for a longer period without trial. Nor can the government disregard the law and imprison its opponents without trial. The difficulty is, of course, to ensure that the legislature and government respect the law.

There are several ways in which one can try to ensure that the rights of citizens listed in a bill of rights are respected. One is by **convention**. The earliest bill of rights was an English statute of 1689. Since in England (now Britain) the legislature is sovereign, it has the legal power to disregard the rights listed in the bill, such as the right to free speech in Parliament. But in practice the legislature and government have respected these rights.

Another way of enforcing rights is through an **international treaty**. A state may agree to a treaty that gives citizens certain rights and sets up a court to judge whether they have been respected by the government of the state, its legislature or its judges. This is what happened with the European Convention on Human Rights, which came into force in 1953. For instance, the European Convention gives a person charged with a crime the right to a fair trial. Anyone who objects that he has not had a fair trial in, say, Britain can complain to the European Court of Human Rights in Strasbourg. If the court thinks that he has not been fairly tried, the state in which the trial has taken place has a duty to put the matter right, if necessary by changing the law.

But the simplest way of protecting fundamental rights is to **give the courts** of the country in which the rights are to be respected **the power to enforce them**. That is what happens in the USA, where the written constitution itself lists the rights to be protected, for instance the right not to be deprived of property without due process of law (see Chapter 4). It is for the American courts to decide whether a law passed by Congress or a decision of the federal government has wrongly deprived someone of his property.

Supporters of legislative sovereignty object to this way of enforcing rights because it gives **too much power to judges**. If property rights are listed in the bill of rights judges have the last word on how far that protection should extend. They decide on what terms the state can expropriate private property. This, the trustful school argues, is a political question which, in a democratic society, should be left to the legislature.

But in most countries, even democratic countries, governments and legislatures cannot always be trusted to respect basic human rights. So the judges may be the lesser of two evils.

Judicial review

Judicial review is also a way of limiting the freedom of governments. Judges can be given power to **review acts of the government** (decisions by ministers, public bodies and officials) **or even acts of the legislature** (statutes) to see if they conform to law. As we have seen, the separation of powers, federalism and bills of rights can hardly work effectively unless some independent body has the power to declare laws invalid if they are against the constitution.

The judges are the obvious people to do this, if only because every country needs a body of impartial and independent judges to decide ordinary disputes which do not turn on the limits of state power. But in a society where judges are mistrusted, or are not independent enough, a different body could be chosen. In France, a constitutional council decides whether proposed laws are against the constitution.

Even if nobody has the power to decide that a statute is against the constitution, the rule of law is more secure if citizens can **challenge the decisions of ministers, officials and public bodies** before the courts. For instance, it is important that citizens should be able to challenge a decision to give planning permission for a new road. In some countries the ordinary courts have the power to do this, but in others, such as France and Germany, special administrative courts hear these cases. Sometimes the proposed decision can be challenged in advance, sometimes only after the event.

The usual grounds of challenge are that the decision was **not authorised by any law**, or that the person who made it **abused his powers** in doing so. This may be because he was corrupt or biased, or because he took account of things that he should not have, or left out of account things that he should have considered. For example he approved of the road because he knew it would annoy a political enemy, or he failed to consider the effect the road would have on drainage in the area.

The trustful school of thought thinks that the government should be free, provided it does not break the law, to govern in whatever way it thinks best. It would prefer to keep judicial review to a minimum, since it is expensive and causes delay in reaching and carrying out decisions. The sceptical school thinks it more important that the government and public bodies should reach the right, or at any rate defensible, decisions even at the expense of cost and delay.

The argument between trust and scepticism runs through public law from beginning to end.

4
Property

A great deal of law is about property. People feel more secure if they own things; if, within limits, they can do what they like with them; and if the things they own cannot be taken away from them without their consent. One of the main aims of law is to increase people's sense of security, and one of the ways it does this is by recognizing and protecting property rights.

What is property? Anything that has a **money value** and can be cashed or exchanged counts as property: land, buildings, furniture, vehicles, leases, money, shares, copyrights. For something to be property it has to be possible for someone **to have an exclusive right** to it. There cannot be property in something like the air which we have to share with others whether we like it or not.

Reasons for protecting property

So the first question about property has to be whether it is right for the state to protect an exclusive right of this sort, rather than to insist that people share things. One reason for **protecting private property** is that this helps those who own it to be more **independent**. For this purpose there have to be rules that lay down **who owns each thing** — who has the best right to it. It is true that not all states want their citizens to be independent; but those that do not nevertheless protect property owned by the state and other public bodies. They also find it convenient to give people some limited rights to private property, since that encourages them to work harder and be more productive.

Another reason for protecting property is to make sure that economic and domestic life can be carried on **without too much interference** by others. A viable economy and home life is possible only if people are not free to take things from others without their leave. It is better that those who are **in control of things** (who have what the law calls possession), **should remain in control** and be free to use the thing broadly as they choose until a court decides otherwise. So, alongside rules that lay down who owns what, there have to be rules protecting possession and discouraging even owners from taking the law into their own hands.

A third reason for having a law of property is that property law can be used to **create assets** of a sort that did not exist before, such as patents and copyrights, and in that way reward originality and stimulate enterprise.

In practice all societies have a law of property that lays down who owns what and gives exclusive rights to the owners of the thing owned. Certainly the spread of property that results from these rules may be unjust; some may have too much and others too little. But property law is based on the view that even an unjust spread of the resources available to a society is better than a free-for-all.

The law of property has to answer three key questions. What counts as property? Who is to own what — what justifies giving a particular person an exclusive right to a particular thing? And how are property rights to be protected?

WHAT COUNTS AS PROPERTY?

First, what things should count as property? Property must have some value; and things have value only if they **can be controlled**; and the control, for which the legal term is **possession**, can be physical or legal. Can one own fish in the sea? Not if they are swimming about freely. But if I am fishing in a place where I have the right to fish and have caught fish in my net I have them in my control and so I can own them. What about those I have almost netted when your boat cuts my net? Can I then claim that you let my fish get away? That is a matter of dispute.

Of physical things, the most basic sorts of property are land, including the buildings on it, and goods such as clothes, furniture and vehicles. The person who occupies land may, if challenged, be able to defend it with his strong right arm or his gun. The same is true of physical goods. But the value of land and goods increases if they are legally secure.

Other sorts of property that can be physically controlled have little or no value apart from what law gives it. Take money. The metal in the coins or the paper in the banknotes is worth hardly anything. Money is worth what it claims to be worth only because the law gives it that worth. Law forces those who are owed money to accept the coins or notes in payment, and gives the state a monopoly (an exclusive right) of issuing money.

Property created by the law

All these are examples of property based on physical control, or physical control plus a legal monopoly. But sometimes the law itself creates the control needed for property to exist. Copyright is an example. The author of an original article or novel who wants to sell it is in a bad position if, when he loses physical control of what he has written by handing over the manuscript or tape, he no longer has the exclusive right to have it reproduced. That he keeps the ownership of his manuscript or tape is not much consolation if other people can copy it as they please.

Copyright, which is a legal invention, gives the author a monopoly of the right to reproduce and copy the original. This right lasts only for a limited period, but while it lasts it gives the author the control necessary for copyright to be a type of property of some value. For example, he can sell it.

There are, however, **objections to monopolies**. It is true that some monopolies, like the state monopoly of issuing money, are necessary, because it would be dangerous to give a private individual the power to issue money. And it is true that every form of property gives the owner an exclusive right of some sort. I have an exclusive right to my apartment. But that does not give me a monopoly of apartment ownership, for there are other apartments that people can buy. If they could only buy an apartment from me, that would give me a monopoly, and I could hold them to ransom. So we need to be cautious about admitting new forms of property in, let us say, computer programs. There is a case for rewarding original work, but it has to be set against the drawback of denying free access to what has been created. Should there be property, for example, in a genetically engineered cell?

Another sort of property that can be created without physical control consists in **rights under contracts** (see Chapter 5), such as an employee's right to a salary or a seller's right to be paid the price of something he has sold. This sort of property gives the employee or seller an exclusive right, because the payment has to be made to him and no one else. It is of value because of the certainty or likelihood that the payment will be made. Its value is, once again, increased by the fact that, if it is not made, the employee or seller can call on the law to enforce it.

Another kind of property of this sort consists of **shares** in companies. Shares are created by a contract between the company and the shareholder by which the shareholder contributes or promises to contribute to the capital of the company. Much of their value lies in the fact that they have a chance of earning dividends if the company prospers, though they are not certain to.

There are other forms of property. Indeed there is no limit to the sorts of property that could in theory be created. In practice there are limits, since sharing has its place in society. For instance it seems right, and fits the idea that the chief aim of the medical profession is to heal the sick, that the inventor of a new method of medical treatment (as opposed to a new drug) should not have property in it. If he did, every doctor who wanted to use the treatment would have to pay for the right to use it. When a new sort of property is proposed, the claim to share and the claim to be rewarded for initiative have to balanced against one another.

WHO OWNS WHAT?

So much for what counts as property. For a system of property law to work, each thing, each item of property, has to be allotted to an owner. The owner is said to 'have the property' in the thing he owns. By 'owner' is meant the **person who has the best right to control the thing in the long run**, though in the short run someone else may have a more immediate right to it. So I can own an apartment though at the moment it is let to you or mortgaged to a building society.

How can we decide who has the best long-term right to this or that bit of property? Several factors need to be taken into account, of which the most important are: rewarding initiative, giving effect to agreements to pay for or transfer things, encouraging trade, and seeing that things are properly looked after.

Most people would agree that the **person who makes something** (makes a table) should own the table. The skill or effort that has gone into making the thing gives them a better claim than anyone else. But if the maker made the thing for someone else the agreement between them will decide who owns it. So, if the table was made by an employee as part of his work the employer usually owns it, because that is what the contract between employer and employee lays down or implies.

Land, the most important resource, is a special case. Though the law of some countries rewards the initiative of the person who first clears land by giving him the ownership of the land cleared, most insist that only the state can grant the ownership of land that has not up to now had a private owner.

Once we have discovered who the original owner of the thing is, it follows, if agreements are to be respected, that **the present owner** will be the person who can trace his right back to the original owner by one or more sales, gifts, etc. The idea is that owning a thing includes the right to pass on the ownership to someone else by agreement. That person can in turn pass the ownership of the thing on to another, and so on in a chain which can continue so long as the thing still exists.

Sometimes, however, the ownership of a thing is **transferred without the owner's consent**. In certain cases this is inevitable. If an owner dies without making a will his property has to be transferred to someone. Who that is must be settled by a rule of law — unless the property is to be taken by the first comer or forfeited to the state, neither of which seems a good idea. The law of intestate succession, which deals with the problem of who is to succeed to the property of those who do not make a will, deals with this difficulty by giving the thing to a close relative — the sort of person who most people would be likely to want to give it to, if they had thought about it and made a will in time.

When the owner loses his ownership without consent

There are also some cases in which the ownership of property is transferred against the owner's will, for example if he cannot pay his creditors and becomes insolvent. In that case arrangements are made for an official to sell his property and distribute the proceeds, up to the amount of his debts, to his creditors. His duty to pay his debts is given priority over his rights as an owner.

These rules for deciding who the original owner of a thing is and who is the present owner seem straightforward enough. But they do not fully meet the aims of encouraging buying and selling and of seeing that property is well looked after. If these aims are to be met the owner will, quite apart from the case of insolvency, sometimes have to be deprived of his ownership without his consent.

As regards **buying and selling**, the difficulty is that someone who wants to buy property may not know whether the person who offers to sell it to him is the owner. He may be a thief or someone who has bought the thing from a thief. How is he to find out?

One answer is that there should be a **register of ownership** that the buyer can consult. In many countries there is a public record of land ownership, a land register, which records who owns what land. That is convenient for the owner, and for anyone who wants to buy the land, or to lend money on the security of a mortgage over the land. Registration of title, as it is called, is convenient and safe because the state guarantees that, with minor exceptions, the person recorded in the register as owner really is the owner.

But for most ordinary goods a public register is too expensive or inconvenient. In the absence of a register someone who wants to buy, say, a lap-top computer has to assume that the person who has it and offers it for sale owns it. Yet clearly he may not. He may have borrowed or hired or stolen the lap-top computer.

Two ideas about ownership, then, compete. One is that **a person cannot be deprived of his ownership without his consent**. This idea gives priority to long-term security. It follows that if I lend or hire my lap-top computer to you or you steal it or find it left in your office and you then sell it to Jane, I can claim it back from Jane. This is true even if Jane thought it was yours and paid for it as if it was. I do not have to pay Jane what she paid for it. When she bought the computer she took the risk that it did not belong to you.

The alternative idea is that when a person **buys something in good faith** the buyer's security has priority over the owner's. On this view Jane is entitled to assume that you own the computer unless she knows or there is something to indicate that you do not (for example it is stamped with my name). It follows that once the computer is handed to her she owns it and it no longer belongs to me. Of course I can claim compensation from you, but that may not be worth much.

A compromise view is that, if I lent or hired the computer to you, and you sell Jane the computer, I lose my ownership; but that I do not lose it if you stole it from me and then sold it to Jane. In the case of loan or hire I part voluntarily with the possession of the computer, and take the risk that you will sell it. In the second I do not.

Someone has to bear the risk that the seller may not own the thing. Many countries treat the owner's security as the dominant aim of property law, so far as ordinary goods are concerned. But as regards money and, to a lesser extent, documents like cheques (called **negotiable instruments**), law treats the security of the person to whom the money or cheque is transferred by way of payment as more important. A person who is paid money is therefore in a better position than the buyer of ordinary goods. He usually cannot know whether the person who pays him owns the money or has stolen it. But once he is paid, he becomes the owner of the money, even if it was stolen, so long as he does not know that it was stolen. It would hamper trade and private dealing too much if we had to take the risk that people who pay us are not entitled to the money that they pay with.

That is one of the ways in which an owner can lose ownership of a thing without his consent. Ownership can also be lost through the **passage of time**. Suppose that a thing, say a table, is taken from or lost by the owner and that he does not take steps to recover it. The taker or finder takes possession of it and treats it as his. After a period, which varies in different countries from a few years to as many as 30, most systems of law transfer the ownership of the thing to the new possessor. Or they lay down (what amounts to the same thing in practice) that the owner cannot recover the thing from the present possessor. The idea is that it is better for someone who is interested in the thing, even if they have taken it dishonestly, to own it rather than someone who over a long period has taken no interest in it. This can apply even when there is a public register of ownership, such as the land register. The registered owner who takes no steps to recover possession of his land over a long period may find that he has lost the ownership of it.

THE PROTECTION OF PROPERTY RIGHTS

So much for the problem of deciding who owns what, and how ownership can be lost. In protecting property rights law has two main aims: to protect the owner and to protect the possessor. Let us take the owner first. The owner is the person with the best long-term right to the possession of the thing; so there are two ways of protecting him.

One is to give the owner a right to claim the thing from anyone who cannot show that he is entitled to keep it temporarily, for instance because he has hired it from the owner. The second way is to **give the right to claim** not to the owner but **to the person who is immediately entitled to possess the thing,** who may or may not be the owner. This second way protects the owner in the long run. The owner is always entitled to possess the thing in the long run, but not always in the short run; for example a lessee is entitled to possess the flat he has leased until the lease runs out. The difference is one of legal technique. Some countries adopt the first technique, some the second.

If the owner establishes his claim, it does not always follow that the court will order the person in possession to hand over the thing to him. Sometimes courts order a similar thing or an equivalent in money to be handed over instead. The rules vary a bit from one country to another. If the thing is unique, in the way that a plot of land or a painting by a famous artist is unique, a court will almost certainly order it to be handed over; but if it is a vehicle or some other mass-produced item, some countries are satisfied with ordering an equivalent in kind or money to be given over.

The protection of possession

So much for the way in which the law protects the owner. But to protect the owner is not enough if the law is to promote social peace and harmony. To discourage people from taking the law into their own hands, from resorting to self-help, the person who possesses a thing without owning it also needs to be protected. So all systems of law protect possession as well as ownership.

The legal idea of **possession is a refined version of control**, and takes account to some extent of custom and social convention. For example, a host possesses the chair in which a guest is sitting at table because, although the guest is actually using the chair, by convention it is for the host to decide who should sit where.

Laws that protect a possessor typically lay down that **a person who is dispossessed of a thing can get it back from the person who took it**. So, if you take the motorcycle I have been riding without asking me, you dispossess me and I can take it back without asking you, provided I don't use force. If someone else took the motorcycle from you, he dispossessed you in turn and you can claim it back from him though you don't own it. And if I use force to get the motorcycle back from you there are countries where the law would make me return it to you before I can claim it back from you, even if I own the cycle.

These countries treat the question of who has been wrongfully dispossessed of the thing and who owns it as quite separate. They lay down that the question whether I have wrongfully dispossessed you of the motorcycle has to be decided before the question of whether I own it is decided. This roundabout way of dealing with the matter is meant to discourage people from taking the law into their own hands. But not all legal systems adopt it. Some prefer the simpler method of deciding both issues at the same time.

Protecting ownership makes for long-term stability and protecting possession for short-term stability. Both have a place in a system of property law; but it is not easy to decide on the best way of achieving a balance.

5
Contracts and treaties

This chapter is about the part law plays in enforcing agreements. The main agreements it is concerned with are those between individuals and between states. Legally binding agreements between individuals, or between a state and an individual, are **contracts**. Binding agreements between states are **treaties**.

There are two main points to be discussed. What agreements should be treated as legally binding contracts or treaties? And if an agreement is legally binding, how should it be enforced?

Agreements

Agreements are important for more than one reason. In many areas of life coming to an agreement with your opponent is the **only practical alternative to coming to blows**. This is true in international relations, where the choice is often between making war and making a treaty. It was once equally true of conflicts within states, from vendettas and political clashes to full-scale civil war. The role of agreements in settling these conflicts within states is now less, but has by no means vanished.

A second reason why agreements are important, even outside the law, is that they provide a way of **binding people to do something in future**. To bind yourself to do something in future is to promise to do it. Many promises take the form of an agreement between the person who makes the promise and the person to whom it is made. Any form of economic life beyond the most primitive depends on our being able to rely on people to keep their promises. We must know that people who undertake to work or supply goods or build houses or pay when they have been given credit will do so. We can know this only if the agreements in which they promise to do these things are regarded as binding.

People who make an agreement are called the **parties** to the agreement. An agreement is a guarantee of future conduct only if there is some way of enforcing it. What ways are available, apart from law, for persuading parties to keep their agreements?

By and large people regard themselves as **morally bound** to do what they promise. In fact that is the point of making a promise. Of course there are exceptions. Sometimes it is impossible to carry out the promise; or it should not have been made in the first place — think of a terrorist's promise to plant a bomb in a supermarket. Our moral sense is the first motive for keeping promises. To it is added a regard for our own **self-interest**. We benefit from being thought reliable; and if we want to be thought reliable we have to keep our promises, or show good reason why we did not.

The argument for keeping promises is still stronger if I make you a promise in return for a benefit, or promised benefit, to myself. If I agree to sell you my house I must, if I want to get the price, be willing to transfer the house to you when you pay. Unless you know that I will do this, you won't pay. But how can you know that I will transfer the house to you if you do pay? For it may suit me to break the agreement. Suppose that, since agreeing to sell to you, I have received a better offer. A sense of honour or long-term self-interest may persuade me to transfer the house to you all the same. But can you rely on this?

Even if you know me well you cannot take the chance. You need to be sure of getting the house you have chosen to buy; and that is possible only if the agreement for sale is legally binding, in which case I shall be compelled, if necessary by a court order, to transfer the house to you. **Nothing short of compulsion will meet the case**, and **only the state**, which stands behind the court order, **has the necessary force at its disposal**.

In less important cases, like buying a lawn-mower, it may not be essential to compel the seller to deliver the particular lawn-mower he has sold, provided the buyer **gets an equivalent** lawn-mower or the money to buy one.

Sometimes, again, it is impossible to enforce the agreement, for instance when a singer who was due to sing at a concert has failed to turn up on the day agreed and it is too late to arrange for it to be held on another day. In that case it is still important, if agreements are to be respected, that the singer should know that he or she will have to **pay compensation** (the legal term is '**damages**') for breaking the agreement — unless there was a good reason for it to be broken, such as illness.

Whether the agreement is to be enforced as agreed (the house), or an equivalent given (the substitute lawn-mower) or compensation paid (the singer), **law is needed** to make sure that agreements are by and large respected and that those who do not respect them can be forced to make good the loss. Economic life would soon decline or even grind to a halt if contracts for employment, sale, hire, loan, insurance and many others did not have the force of law. So would international relations and international trade, which depend both on trading contracts and on the binding force of treaties.

One reason, then, why some agreements have to be made legally binding is as a guarantee that they will be carried out or that, if they are not, a substitute will be provided or compensation paid. There is a second reason. By ensuring, up to a point, that agreements will be kept, law creates economic assets. Your legal right to the house you have bought from me is a form of property (see Chapter 4), even before the house has been transferred to you. It is an asset that you can use to obtain a loan on mortgage. You can do this in return for giving the bank or society that lends you the money a guarantee that if necessary the house can be resold to repay the loan. The bank or society that has lent the money can in turn use the fact that it is entitled to have the loan repaid as an asset of its own, on which it can raise or lend money, and so on.

WHICH AGREEMENTS ARE LEGALLY BINDING?

'Agreements ought to be be kept'. This saying forms one of the foundations of international law. But if it means that the law should enforce **every agreement we make**, it cannot be taken literally. In practice, not all agreements are contracts or treaties; nor should they be. There must be an extra reason for the state (through the courts) or the international community to back up an agreement rather than leave it to the parties to decide what to do if it is broken.

Even the strictest moralist does not think that the law should enforce all the agreements we make. Some are **not serious commitments**. If we agree that I will take you on holiday if I can, I have not made a firm promise. Other agreements are too **vague** to be easily enforced by a court ('if you don't pester me, I'll pay for your computing course').

Yet other agreements, though they amount to definite commitments, are too **private** to be the concern of the law. An agreement to accept a social invitation may be perfectly serious, but should the courts be asked to enforce it? Most of us assume that there should be a private sphere of life from which the state is excluded. Where exactly to draw the line is, of course, a difficult question.

Many civil law systems hold that if an agreement is **serious, definite and meant to be legally binding** it is legally enforceable. Common law systems, on the other hand, generally require something more. Their point of view is derived from the model of business dealings. **Bargains**, in which each party stands to gain something from the agreement, can be enforced, just because each party stands to gain from them. And an agreement can be enforced by a party who stands to lose if it isn't enforced, because he has **relied** on it. But a promise to do someone a favour or to make a gift, however seriously meant, cannot be enforced, unless the promise is made by a written deed, signed and witnessed.

Here is an example. Suppose you have rented a flat and the landlord has told you that, as you are in financial difficulties, he will let you off the rent for 3 months. Later he finds that he needs the money, and demands the rent for those 3 months all the same. His agreement to let you off was **seriously meant, but it wasn't a bargain**. He did not stand to benefit from the agreement. So from a common law point of view the agreement is not binding, though from a civil law point of view it is. The agreement would be binding in common law if to your landlord's knowledge you had lost the chance of moving to cheaper lodgings because **you relied on his keeping his promise**.

Before the common law view is dismissed as hard-hearted, we must note that all legal systems, both civil and common law, are uneasy about enforcing promises of gifts. One device that some civil law systems adopt is to insist that a promise of a gift should be **in writing** or even that it should be made in front of a **notary** (an official who specializes in legal documents). This is to make sure that the giver has really thought about the consequences of making the gift. In fact in France, outside business deals, no agreement can be enforced as a contract unless there is **some written evidence** of its making.

Written evidence is certainly not a cast-iron test of a commitment to being legally bound, because we often make promises in private letters that we do not mean to bind us in law. But to put a promise or agreement in writing is some evidence of serious commitment. Writing has other advantages. It provides proof of what was agreed and helps to avoid disputes about whether there has really been an agreement (see Chapter 8). International treaties are in practice always made in writing and signed by the parties.

The bargain approach

As mentioned, common law systems tend to play down the need for written evidence but to require that, unless there is a formal written document (a **deed**), agreements should be enforced only if each party to them stands to gain something from the agreement. This approach is based on the model of a business deal, a market transaction, which is very often not in writing but is meant to benefit both parties.

On the bargain approach the law should enforce deals from which both sides think they will benefit, even if one is really paying too much or too little; but it should not enforce agreements where the benefit is entirely on one side. The assumption is that when people promise gifts or favours they do not mean to be legally bound to carry out the promise unless they put it in a form that leaves no room for doubt. Or if they do intend to be bound, they need to be protected against being held to rash promises from which they derive no benefit.

It is therefore only in borderline cases that there is a real difference in practice between the common law and the civil law view about enforceable agreements. But there is a difference in outlook. The civil law is more moralistic, the common law more down to earth and more business-oriented.

The singer and the wedding

Even though legal systems agree (broadly) about what agreements are enforceable, it can be difficult to decide in a borderline case on which side of the line the agreement falls. Here is an (invented) set of facts that falls on the borderline. I invite a friend who sings in a band to sing at my daughter's wedding. She does not ask to be paid and I do not promise to pay her. I hire a piano and an accompanist for the occasion. Although the singer knows I have done this, she does not turn up, and does not let me know that she is not coming. Has she broken a contract?

It is not at first sight clear whether she seriously meant to bind herself to sing at the wedding. The fact that she is a friend of the family counts in favour of her promise being seriously meant. So does the fact that she knew that I had hired a piano and accompanist, for this means that she knew I was taking her promise seriously, and incurring expense on the strength of it.

On the bargain approach, however, the fact that she is a friend of the family counts against there being a contract. Friends do not usually bargain with one another; and is not this the sort of social arrangement that the state should not intrude into?

That the singer is not to be paid also counts, on the bargain approach, against a contract. A promise to do someone a favour without being paid is not a promise of a gift, but it is similar.

But, though the agreement with the singer did not mention payment and was between friends that is not a knock-down argument against our having made a contract, even on the bargain approach. I have incurred the expense of hiring the piano and accompanist; and, as she knows that I have done this, I can argue that when she said she would sing it was implied that I would pay the cost of hiring the piano and accompanist. In fact (I can argue) we impliedly struck a bargain that she would sing for nothing and I would provide the piano and accompanist.

There certainly can be implied contracts. If I board a bus it is implied that I will pay the fare to my destination; the bus driver does not need to ask me whether I am prepared to pay the fare. If I pay the fare to Kensington, which is on the bus route, it is implied that the bus company will take me there. I do not need to ask the bus driver whether he is willing to take me there. But it is difficult to think that the singer and I made a **bargain** along the lines suggested. She would have had no complaint had I changed my mind and decided that there was after all to be no singing at the wedding. Financially, she would have lost nothing if that had happened, though she would have lost a chance of being heard by the guests.

This example shows that even a simple agreement can begin to look quite complex when we try to see if it is a contract.

HOW CAN CONTRACTS AND TREATIES BE ENFORCED?

For contracts, like other legal arrangements, to be enforced the state must have **sufficient force** at its disposal. The enforcement of treaties also depends on state power, because it is states that have to give effect to treaties, both internally and externally.

Given state force, courts can order parties to an agreement to carry it out (transfer the house that has been sold), or to provide a substitute for what was promised (a truck similar to the one sold), or to pay compensation for not doing what was agreed (damages against the singer for failing to turn up and sing). The law can also allow a party to withdraw from an agreement which the other party is clearly not going to carry out. If the plumber who has agreed to repair my leaking cistern delays too long in coming to my apartment to carry out urgent repairs I can withdraw from my contract with him ('**rescind the contract**') and get another plumber instead. If I have made an advance payment for the rent of a holiday villa and the owner does not make it available as agreed I can recover the advance payment ('**claim restitution**').

These **remedies**, as they are called, reflect one of two ideas. One is that **a legally binding agreement must be carried out**. If it is not, state force should be used to see that it is, or that the other party is put in as good a position as if it had been. Legal systems vary about whether the party to whom the promise has been made is entitled to insist that the court orders the contract to be performed **as agreed** (awards '**specific performance**'), assuming that it is still possible to perform it. On the moralist approach, which civil law systems tend to adopt, an order for performance should be the standard remedy against someone who breaks a contract. On the bargain approach, when money will put the other party in an equally good position, the court need not order specific performance.

The other idea that underlies the remedies mentioned is that, if someone is justified in withdrawing from an agreement, he should if possible be put in **as good a position as if he had never made it in the first place**. I should not lose because I made an agreement with you that you failed to carry out.

When a contract is broken, it sometimes seems right to put the party who suffers in as good a position as if the other party had kept his agreement. In other cases it seems right to put the party who suffers in as good a position as if he had not made the agreement in the first place.

In the case of a builder who fails to do the work agreed with me the first alternative seems right. He should pay me enough to get the work that he promised to do, but did not carry out, done by another builder. But in the case of the singer who fails to turn up, the second seems the right way to compensate me. She should pay the expenses that I have incurred to no purpose. But it is not easy to explain the difference.

The remedies for breaking treaties are to some extent similar to those for breaking contracts. Many treaties provide for **arbitration** and give arbitrators power to award compensation. Clearly treaties cannot be enforced in the straightforward way in which state courts enforce contracts. Often there is no court that has power to enforce a treaty or to give damages if it is broken. In spite of that, treaties are by and large observed. In their own self-interest states respect them and use state power to enforce them internally, and sometimes externally.

This can be true even when treaties seriously cut down the power of a state to act as it sees fit. Various treaties, including the Charter of the United Nations, lay down that, though states may use force in self-defence, they may not use or threaten force against one another's territory. However powerful the reason for it, **aggression is forbidden**.

To outlaw state aggression, which is a development of the twentieth century, is to adopt a simple test that avoids inquiring whether any particular act of aggression was morally justified. It rejects the old idea that some wars of aggression are just (wars in self-defence are another matter). The new principle has been surprisingly successful. Relatively few states have invaded the territory of others in the last 50 years, and most of the invasions have failed, at least in the long run. But the steps to be taken when one state invades another are not laid down in detail by international law and are not settled by any court. They depend on the political and military possibilities, as seen by the Security Council of the United Nations, which has the legal power to decide what to do, and by the governments concerned, which have to contribute whatever forces are needed for the purpose.

International treaties are less effective when the tests they propose are vague. This has proved to be true of various **treaties intended to protect human rights**. Unlike the question whether one state has invaded the territory of another, the question whether a state has violated human rights is nearly always debatable. This type of law can be enforced only when the states concerned accept the power of a court to decide whether the law has been violated. This is what has happened under the European Convention of Human Rights, which many European countries have accepted. The European Court of Human Rights decides whether a member state has violated human rights.

Law has an important part to play in enforcing agreements, **provided the agreements are clear and that their enforcement is backed by morality and self-interest**.

6
Crimes

The state and private vengeance

All systems of law try to keep wrongdoing, or disruptive behaviour, within limits. Otherwise people cannot feel secure. Complete security is not possible or desirable, but if people feel too insecure they '**take the law into their own hands**'. They arrange to beat, lynch, shun or expel those whose behaviour they find obnoxious. They feel the need for law and, if the state does not provide it, make up their own informal and often vicious version of it.

For example, in a society where there is no central authority, or the central authority is weak, killings lead to **feuds** between families and clans. But the families and clans are not impartial. They are judges in their own cause. Retaliation by one side is seldom thought just by the other. The feud goes on and may last for generations.

So when the state is strong enough it has good reason to intervene and try to enforce decent standards of conduct. It has a better chance than victims and their families of being seen as fair and of reducing private vengeance to a minimum. The state (and the international community) try to deal with disruptive behaviour in a way which aims at being both consistent and impartial. They decide what behaviour is so disruptive that they must intervene. They make this behaviour a **legal wrong**.

But these legal wrongs **do not cover everything that is regarded as wrong in private life**. Telling lies is usually wrong, but only special sorts of lies, such as perjury in a court of law, or lies that have specially bad consequences, like defrauding customers, are legal wrongs.

On the other hand legal wrongs include some behaviour that is not thought wrong, or not seriously wrong, in private life. Exceeding the speed limit on the open road, when there is no danger ahead, is a case in point. To exceed the speed limit is made a legal wrong because it is often, though not always, dangerous to drive at more than a certain speed. Given that, it is in practice simpler and cheaper to impose a blanket ban than for the driver and the court to work out in each case what the safe speed was in the circumstances. The driver who exceeds the speed limit when it is safe to do so has his freedom limited in the general interest. But is this fair?

Crimes and torts

In secular systems of law legislators, government ministers and judges decide what amounts to legal wrongdoing. The wrongs they define are of two sorts, crimes and torts. **Crimes** like murder and burglary are treated as wrongs against the state even though the victim is a private person; and those who commit them, if convicted, are punished by the state. **Torts** (also called delicts), like running someone over by negligent driving, are treated as wrongs against individuals. Those harmed by them can claim money from the wrongdoer as compensation; but unless they take the initiative the state does not help them to get compensation. If, however, they do take the initiative, the state provides machinery (courts, judges and bailiffs) so that the wrongdoer will be forced to pay up.

Although the state recognizes these two types of wrong, crimes and torts, the same conduct can be made a crime or a tort or both. An example of conduct that is both a crime and a tort is obtaining money by fraud or, if it injures someone else, dangerous driving. When conduct is both a crime and a tort the two wrongs are treated as separate. So the wrongdoer may both be punished and have to pay compensation to the person harmed by his conduct.

Why does the state use **two different methods** of keeping wrongdoing within limits? The reason is that sometimes (e.g. when injury is caused in a motor accident) the victim has a strong incentive to get the wrongdoer to pay for the harm. The law of torts then gives the victim the right to take the initiative in claiming compensation. But at other times individuals have little interest in seeing the law enforced, or the chances of getting compensation are small. Most thieves, even if caught, are not worth suing; yet theft makes people insecure. The state therefore takes the initiative on behalf of the community. It makes theft a crime; and through the police, prosecutors, judges and prison officials it pursues and punishes the thief.

Crimes and torts look **both to the future and to the past**. They are meant to deter people from doing things in future that are seen as undesirable. They also seek to provide a remedy (punishment or compensation) if the threat hasn't worked. This chapter is concerned with crimes, the next with torts. I shall discuss two issues about crimes. What **type of conduct** does and should the state make criminal? And **under what conditions** is it fair to hold someone guilty of a crime in a particular case?

WHAT TYPE OF CONDUCT AMOUNTS TO A CRIME?

First, then, as to the type of conduct that is a crime. Legal systems largely agree about this. The state targets

(1) conduct that by causing or threatening harm creates insecurity;
(2) conduct that causes offence, and
(3) conduct that undermines the smooth working of society, its government and economy.

Laws make conduct criminal if by **causing or threatening harm** it creates a sense of insecurity. What counts as harm depends to some extent on what each society thinks is objectionable. But behaviour that strikes at people's lives and bodies, their property or the safety of the whole community is everywhere regarded as harmful.

To begin with people's **lives and bodies**, all countries make it a crime intentionally to kill another person (murder) or to wound them. It is also a crime to threaten someone in such a way that they think that they are about to be killed or wounded (assault). Equally or more disturbing is forcing someone to have sexual intercourse against their will (rape).

The state takes the view that these inroads on life and bodily security are too disruptive to be left solely to the victim or his family to take legal action. We all have an interest in other people not being murdered, wounded or raped, not only ourselves and our families. In practice, however, the state and its officials often cannot prosecute the wrongdoer unless the victim (for example the woman raped) reports what has happened and gives evidence against her attacker. Indeed, they may not want to prosecute unless this is what the victim wants.

The crimes mentioned are offences against our bodies or persons. Less disruptive but still of serious concern are offences against **property**. Property (see Chapter 4) is an element of stability in people's lives, whether they are rich or poor. Theft is in all countries a crime and other ways of taking or threatening to take other people's money or goods without their consent, such as fraud, forgery, and blackmail, are treated as crimes too. Intentionally to destroy or damage someone else's property is also criminal.

Conduct that alarms and threatens to undermine society is not confined to harming persons or property. **Public security** is also important. Treason confronts the state and the community with the danger of foreign invasion or destabilisation. Public disorder threatens revolution, rioting or at least widespread unrest.

Conduct that does not threaten the safety of people or property may nevertheless **give serious offence**. For example, excessive noise or smell, public nudity and prostitution may create such annoyance that the state has to intervene. Offence is not quite the same as harm, since what is offensive depends entirely on how people react to the behaviour in question. If society became nudist public nudity would no longer give offence and there would no longer be a case for making it a crime.

Regulatory crimes

Apart from behaviour that threatens persons, property and public security there are in modern systems of law a whole range of crimes that consist in breaking regulations. They can be called **regulatory crimes**. They work by imposing fines on people whose behaviour threatens something of value to the community: health, road safety, the environment, the working of the courts, the welfare of employees and so on. It can be a crime, for instance, to drive or trade without a licence, to sell stale food, to pollute a river, to interfere with a witness in a lawsuit, to describe goods for sale in a misleading way, and to bribe an official. These actions indirectly threaten our security but they are made crimes mainly to ensure that the services on which a modern society depends run smoothly. A private individual would seldom be interested in seeing that these regulations were enforced. So the state steps in.

So far there is general agreement about the sort of things that should be made crimes, though the details differ from country to country. Two other types of conduct that are sometimes made criminal are controversial. They are paternalistic and purely moral crimes.

Doubtful crimes

Sometimes the state in making conduct a crime behaves like an old-fashioned parent. The idea behind **paternalistic** crimes is that people need to be protected against themselves. Certainly most of us would agree that **some people** need this protection **some of the time**. For example, it is everywhere a crime to have sexual relations with young children or people who are mentally ill even with their consent. Only the minimum age of consent varies from one country to another. The young and the mentally ill are not mature or sensible enough to decide for themselves whether to consent to sex.

It is more difficult to say whether the state should intervene **to prevent adults from**, say, **taking drugs**. In most countries it is a crime to supply certain drugs, such as cannabis and heroin, and it is often a crime even for adults to possess or consume them. The thinking behind this is that taking these drugs, at least the hard drugs, tends in the long run to deprive people of control over their lives. So freedom to take drugs may later undermine their ability to make choices. Drug addiction also throws a burden on other people, and on the medical services, which have to look after addicts when they are hooked.

On the other hand it is nowhere, so far as I know, a crime to sell, possess or smoke cigarettes, though these can be addictive, can cause a range of illnesses and can burden the medical services. In some countries the state insists that the manufacturer or seller should warn the buyer of the dangers of smoking, but it does not go so far as to forbid smoking.

Whether there is any real difference between nicotine and other drugs, or whether the explanation is that the manufacturers of cigar-ettes have more political clout than the makers of drugs, is not clear. No doubt when someone does not realise the risk they are running **a warning is often justified**. This applies not just to smoking cigarettes but to activities like pot-holing, where those who get into trouble put both themselves and rescuers at risk.

But is the state justified in **forbidding** adults from harming them-selves, or risking their own lives, as opposed to harming others or exposing others to risk? Some countries make it a crime to attempt suicide or maim oneself, others do not. The case for making these things crimes is less strong now that states have given up (or should have given up) the idea that a country needs a large, healthy population to fight wars.

The other doubtful type of crime is the **purely moral offence**. I use this term to refer to such things as homosexuality and bigamy (marriage by a person who is already married). The criminal law of most countries allows homosexuality in some circumstances (between consenting adults) and some countries allow polygamy (having more than one wife or husband). In other countries, however, they are or have until recently been strictly forbidden.

The sense in which these crimes are **purely moral** is that they offend people in a different way from the crimes that create physical insecurity, like assaults, or physical offence, like excessive noise and smells. The people they offend regard these **lifestyles as morally** rather than physically **offensive**. The point they are making is that they do not want to live in a society in which these things are freely permitted.

But, apart from the fact that many people do not share these views, the attitude of those who object raises another problem. To what extent are people who would prefer to live in a certain moral environment entitled to force others to conform to their views? Would it be right for vegetarians to insist that the rest of society gave up eating meat? Does the answer depend on whether they are in a majority?

I have so far concentrated on state crimes; but there are also **international crimes**, like state aggression against another state, piracy, hijacking and genocide. These are forms of behaviour by governments or individuals that threaten the international community and its system of communications. They do so in much the same way that state crimes threaten the security of citizens.

WHEN IS IT FAIR TO HOLD SOMEONE GUILTY OF A CRIME?

So much for the sort of behaviour that the state does or should make criminal. For someone to be guilty of a crime he must obviously have done what the state forbids. It would be unfair to punish someone who had not broken the law. To be stamped a criminal is, at any rate if the crime is serious, to suffer disgrace. Before anyone is held up to shame in this way, it seems fair that he should have known, or at least been able to find out, what the law forbade. And he must have been able to avoid breaking the law.

Should we go further and say that it is only fair to punish someone when he **intended** to do what the law forbade? Or is it enough that he **negligently** broke the law, through not taking enough trouble to keep it? Most countries demand some form of fault, either intention or negligence, before anyone is convicted of a crime, apart from regulatory crimes. But they differ in their view of what sort of negligence is criminal.

All these points concern fairness to the person charged. This has to be balanced against the need to reduce to a minimum harms that menace the security of citizens and the stability of a society. The points about fairness need to be gone through one by one.

Did the person charged do what the law forbade?

To show that someone is guilty of a crime the state must prove that he did what the law forbade. Otherwise criminal punishment would be quite arbitrary. The government could punish any behaviour, such as wearing earrings, of which it happened to disapprove, even though it had never gone to the trouble of making a law against it. What the law forbids depends on the definition of the crime; and crimes are mostly defined in codes or statutes, though in some countries judges define them.

Homicide is a good example to take. One form of homicide (murder) is probably the most serious crime; but almost any other crime could be chosen to illustrate the idea of doing what the criminal law forbids.

Homicide is killing another human being. The state's aim in making homicide a crime is to prevent killing. But what is it to kill another person? To kill someone means to **cause his death**. But it is not always easy to decide what amounts to causing another person's death. Suppose I stab Tom. Tom is taken to hospital and given the wrong medical treatment. He dies, though the right treatment would have saved his life.

Have I killed him? He would not have died had I not stabbed him. But does it follow that I killed him? The stab wound does not have to be the **only cause** of Tom's death, but it must be **a cause**; and we have plenty of practice in everyday life in picking out the causes of events.

How can we decide if I have killed Tom? Would it make a

difference if the medical treatment seemed right at the time, though in retrospect, because of an allergy from which he suffered, it was mistaken? Or if the treatment was obviously mistaken, even at the time? These are questions to be answered in the light of common sense.

When killing is permissible

Neither law nor morality always forbids us to kill another person. Sometimes killing is allowed, and it may even be the right thing to kill. I will mention three sorts of case: necessary self-defence and the defence of others; other cases of necessity; and military service.

The most obvious case when killing is permitted is in **necessary self-defence**, or **the defence of other people**. We certainly have a right to defend ourselves against someone who attacks us. If the person who attacks me threatens to kill me, or seriously injure me, the only method of defence may be to kill him; if so, I am entitled to take his life. Surely this must be true even if the person who attacks me is not responsible for his act, for instance if he is mentally disturbed. For I have a right to defend myself, and a duty to defend at least close relatives against attack.

When the person attacked is a stranger to me, the law in most countries gives me a right, though not a duty, to intervene and stop the attack. But from the point of view of the criminal law it makes no difference whether to kill the attacker is a right or a duty. In either case, if I kill the attacker, I have not broken the law.

It is more doubtful whether I have a right to kill **in order to defend my property**, for example to stop a burglar entering my house or taking my car. Life is more valuable than property. On the other hand a person's house is in a sense his territory, and a state can certainly use force to prevent another state encroaching on its territory.

But in general we can kill an attacker only when it is **necessary** to kill him in order to prevent or stop the attack. This means that we have to decide on the spur of the moment how serious the danger is. I am not entitled to kill someone who is merely threatening to hit me. But what if he has a toy gun or knife that I mistake for the real thing? On one view (the objective theory) I am justified in killing only if the threat was real. On another (the subjective theory) I can kill if I genuinely thought the weapon was real. A compromise opinion, for which there is much to be said, is that I am justified in reacting to an apparent threat, even if it turns out later that it was not a real one, if at the time I was justified on the evidence in believing that it was real.

Suppose I kill someone in a fit of temper though I do not think they are threatening to kill or seriously injure me. It turns out, however, that they were. Have I killed them lawfully? If so, I am lucky, in the sort of way in which I am lucky if I shoot at someone without any justification but miss.

There is a more doubtful sort of case in which killing may be justified, or at least excused, though not all systems of law admit this. Sometimes I **have no alternative, if I am to survive**, to killing someone else, though that person is not attacking me. Does that make a difference?

Suppose that, in a shipwreck, I am in a lifeboat that will not hold any more people. I push Jack, who is trying to get in, off the boat, so that he drowns. Or I am in the sea but manage to clamber up and push Jack out, so that I can get in. He drowns. Was I entitled to prefer my life to his? And is there a difference between pushing him off and pushing him out?

If I was entitled to push Jack off he was entitled to push me off. In other words, it was a free-for-all. This does not seem satisfactory. But if I have to sacrifice myself for Jack, he also has to sacrifice himself for me. That does not solve the problem either. Or does the person already in the boat have priority? Remember that, even in a desperate situation, many people care deeply about doing the right thing.

Another case in which we are legally entitled to kill is on **military service**, when ordered to attack the enemy. Modern systems of law, including international law, take the view that the duty to obey military orders is not absolute. A soldier is not entitled to massacre prisoners or commit acts of genocide even if he is ordered by his superior officer to do so. If he is given an illegal order of this sort he is in a difficult position. If he disobeys, he may be shot. To avoid committing an atrocity he may have to risk his own life.

Knowing that the conduct was forbidden

It is generally agreed that, as part of the rule of law, a person should not be punished by the state except for a **crime defined by law in advance**. But crimes can be very vaguely defined. In some countries there are crimes like 'bringing the state into disrepute', or 'corrupting public morals'. Can anyone be certain that what he does will not be held by the courts of his country to come under one of these headings? They seem to give courts too much discretion. But some people argue that if a person does what is morally wrong he cannot complain if what he did turns out to be a crime, though he did not know that it was in advance. He should not have done what he did in any case.

Whether crimes are precisely defined or not, **ignorance** of the law **is in many countries no excuse**. But statutes are published, and it is generally possible to discover (more or less) what is forbidden. One reason why many countries refuse to treat ignorance of the law as an excuse is a practical one. It would often be difficult for the state to prove that a person charged knew about the law he was breaking. If the offender was in fact ignorant, it is simpler to hold him guilty of the crime but to take his ignorance into account when the punishment comes to be fixed. Another reason is that, since law claims to be morally sound, it takes the view that people ought to know, at least in outline, what it requires. These are powerful reasons, but if it is unfair to make someone guilty of a crime when he did not know that what he was doing was against the law, they are not a complete answer.

Being able to do what the law requires

It would not be fair to hold someone guilty of a crime if he could not do what the law required, for instance because he was **too young or mentally unstable** to have full control of himself. At the very least the punishment should be reduced when this is the case. Even if a sane adult breaks the criminal law but can show that she was intolerably provoked into doing so (Joe keeps beating his wife and one day when he is drunk and starts beating her she kills him) this in many systems reduces the seriousness of the crime. The importance of being able to obey the law is discussed further in Chapter 10.

Does fairness require that a person should be convicted of a serious crime **only if he was at fault**? Being at fault means he was to blame for what happened either because he **intended it** or because he could and should have avoided it: it was **negligent** of him not to.

Many people would say that fault is essential. If the person charged was not at fault he did not really do wrong and does not deserve to be punished. Some would go further and say that the punishment should be **in proportion to the fault** — or at any rate not excessive given the degree of fault.

The most serious type of fault is intentionally to do the harm that the law is trying to prevent. For example, a killer can generally be convicted of the most serious form of homicide (murder) only if he intended to kill the victim, or at any rate do him serious injury (e.g. by knifing him). Nearly all countries treat intended killing as worse than other forms of killing.

Why is it worse that the offender intended to do the harm that the law is trying to prevent? Clearly because a person who intends, for example, to kill is deliberately attacking the values that most of us hold and that the law of homicide protects. Defiance of this sort is specially threatening. It is a challenge to the community.

Should negligence be punished?

Does it follow that only those who **defy** the law in this way should be convicted of crimes? That is a possible view. But all modern systems of criminal law make some provision for punishing those who behave **negligently**, though they do not intend to do the harm that the law is trying to prevent.

For example **negligent killing** (of which the English 'manslaughter' is an example) is in one form or another everywhere a crime. But countries vary about what has to be proved to make negligent killing a crime. Some lay down that to be guilty the person charged **must have known** that what he was doing might kill someone and must have gone ahead despite the risk. He must have acted **recklessly**. He was warned not to point a gun at his friend without making sure it was unloaded, but he disregarded the warning and the gun went off and killed the friend.

In others countries a person is guilty of negligent killing if he behaved very foolishly (with **gross negligence**) even if he did not appreciate the risk of killing someone. He thoughtlessly dropped a heavy brick from an upper window, not looking to see if there were pedestrians in the street below. In others, again, **ordinary negligence** (falling below the ordinary standard of care) is enough. The person charged killed someone through speeding in a built-up area.

Is it fair for the state to punish negligence? The argument that it can rightly punish negligence is that a person, without wanting to defy the law, can behave in a way that shows that he **does not care, or not enough, about the welfare of others**. That points to a fault of character, though not as serious a fault as intentional defiance of the law and the values it stands for. It may then be fair to pick on a person who behaves like this and, if he does harm, punish him. But if the punishment is to be in proportion to the fault involved, it should not be as severe as it would be if the offender intended harm. Punishment should take account, among other things, of the degree of fault.

But on the fault theory there is a difficulty about making negligence a crime, at least if the person charged **did not realise** the risks he was exposing others to. To be reckless about whether one kills someone (or does harm in other ways) is to be anti-social, to display bad character. But is this true of someone who did not realise how dangerous his behaviour was? That is debatable. But people who do not realise the risks they are taking are even more dangerous than those who do. To reduce the level of danger, the state may be forced to deter and educate people even if they did not realise they were doing wrong.

Even so, on the fault theory the punishment should reflect how far the person charged realised the risks he was creating and how dangerously he behaved. One way of doing this is to have a special crime, such as manslaughter in English law, that is confined to reckless and grossly negligent killing. Another way is to have a crime of negligent killing in which nothing more than ordinary negligence need be proved, but to punish less those whose fault is less.

What has been said about killing applies to other serious crimes. Crimes that consist in breaking regulations on the other hand sometimes dispense with the need to prove that the person charged was at fault. There are crimes of **strict liability**, like selling liquor to a person under age, where the state need not show that the shopkeeper knew that the buyer was under age or was negligent in not finding this out. How far this sort of liability is fair is discussed in the next chapter, since strict liability is more prominent in tort law than in criminal law.

7
Torts

One way in which the state tries to keep wrongdoing within limits is by giving citizens the right to claim compensation from people who infringe their rights. It does this through the law of **torts**, which in civil law systems are called delicts.

Both these words mean 'wrongs'. Originally there was not much difference between crimes and torts. Today, though the language of wrongs is still used, the behaviour for which people have to pay compensation (for instance damaging someone's car in a road accident) is often wrong only in a weak sense. Either the driver has not been as alert as he should be or, in some countries, he (or more likely his insurance company) is liable to pay even if he was not in any way at fault. He did not intend to do harm, and he was not negligent. In tort law, therefore, we can be responsible although what we have done is not wrong at all, or not seriously wrong.

The aims of tort law

One reason why people can be made to pay compensation for a tort though they may not have done anything wrong is that the law of torts aims to kill two birds with one stone. It tries to **keep wrongdoing under control** and in that way supplement criminal law. It also tries to ensure that people who are harmed by others **get compensation**. In an industrial society accidents multiply, and, if society wants to give its members a reasonable amount of security, the law has to play a part in seeing that those who suffer harm are compensated. The compensation is nearly always in money and is called **damages**.

But these two aims — limiting wrongdoing and providing compensation — clash. If people are to be compensated whenever others harm them then we have to give up, or whittle down, the idea that the person who has to pay compensation must have done something wrong. The law has to compromise. But the form the compromise takes varies from country to country.

Given that the law of tort has this dual aim, it is better not to speak about the person who claims compensation as a 'victim' and the person from whom he claims it as a 'wrongdoer'. Instead I shall talk about the person who has suffered harm as **the plaintiff** (the person who brings a lawsuit) and the person from whom he claims compensation as **the defendant** (the person sued in the lawsuit). We imagine a lawsuit between the two, though in many cases compensation is paid by agreement between the plaintiff and defendant (or their lawyers) without any lawsuit. The advantage of using these terms is that to use them leaves open the question whether a person who harms another can be made to pay compensation only if he was at fault.

The mechanism of tort law is this. It assumes that **plaintiffs have rights** like the right to bodily security and the security of their property. It **makes defendants compensate plaintiffs by paying damages to them if they infringe those rights**. The law of tort also allows a plaintiff to take preventive action, if there is time for it. For instance if his house threatens to collapse because of his neighbour's digging he can get the courts to order the neighbour to respect his property rights and stop the digging. But usually, as with crimes, the law steps in only after the event.

I shall concentrate on two problems in modern tort law. First, **should the defendant be made to compensate the plaintiff only when he was at fault** in bringing about the harm? For example, if a labourer employed on a building site drops a brick on a passer-by and injures him, does his employer, the builder, have to pay damages to the passer-by for the injury even if he was not at fault in supervising the labourer?

Secondly, what rights does and should the law of torts protect? For example, should it compensate a wife if she suffers financial loss and emotional distress when the defendant kills her husband, who was supporting her?

In tackling the first question I assume, for the time being, that the rights that the law of tort protects are those that criminal law gives priority to: the physical safety of people and their property. In practice all systems of tort law protect a wider range of rights than these; but they can be left on one side for the time being.

WHEN IS IT FAIR TO MAKE SOMEONE WHO HARMS ANOTHER PAY THEM COMPENSATION?

The short answer is: at least when by their **fault** they have caused physical harm to another's person or property. Fault, as in criminal law, includes **intention and negligence**. But by what standard does tort law judge whether someone has been negligent?

On the whole tort law adopts the standard of the **average, reasonably competent person**. It is negligent not to be as careful to avoid harm to others as this imaginary person would be. So a driver on the highway must come up to the ordinary standard of driving skill even if he happens to be particularly clumsy. A medical practitioner must keep in mind recent developments in medicine even he happens to have a poor memory or be close to retirement. The standard is objective. It is not morally wrong to be clumsy or to have a poor memory, though it is certainly a defect. But someone who chooses to drive or practice medicine is treated as negligent if they do not come up to the required standard for driving or practising medicine.

On the other hand a person who gives first aid in an emergency, when no doctor was available, would only be expected to **do their best** in the circumstances. The standard is then subjective. (But what about someone who claims to be expert in first aid?). In judging whether a defendant was negligent, systems of tort law apply various mixes of the objective and subjective standards of conduct. On the one hand they want to hold defendants liable only if they were really at fault; on the other hand it would be unfair to the plaintiff to make his claim to compensation depend on the defendant's particular make-up or temperament. There has here, as often in the law, to be a compromise between conflicting aims.

Strict liability

But is there a case for going beyond even the objective standard of negligence and making a defendant pay compensation even though he has not in any sense been at fault? Should the law sometimes impose what is called **strict liability?**

Criminal law, we saw, sometimes makes people pay fines for breaches of regulations designed to protect health, safety, the environment and other things of importance to society. It does this even though they neither intended harm nor were negligent in not preventing it. They are strictly liable without proof of fault.

It is generally thought to be for the public good and, if the fine is not too heavy, not unfair to fine people for breaking regulations even if they were not at fault. One reason is that breaches of regulations do not usually carry with them the public disgrace that crimes such as murder, theft and rape carry. In fact in some countries they are called by a different name, such as 'infringements' instead of 'crimes'. Most people, for instance, think no less of a person who commits a parking offence, unless it causes a serious obstruction.

Systems of tort law, like systems of criminal law, tend to make fault a condition of liability whenever possible. But in tort law, unlike criminal law, **strict liability has, since the industrial revolution, become increasingly common** when there is an accident in which someone is killed or injured. So a person may be held strictly liable for a tort though they have often not committed a wrong in any ordinary sense. Rather, they have exposed other people to a risk, and if harm results, it is thought to be fair and for the public good that they should bear the cost.

When should there be strict liability?

Some cases of strict liability, for example liability for **animals**, have been recognized for a long time. The person who owns or takes charge of a dangerous animal (savage dog, lion) that attacks someone has to compensate the plaintiff, even if he was not at fault in controlling the animal. Though keeping a dangerous animal is not usually forbidden (there are exceptions), keeping it exposes other people to risk. To pay for the harm the animal does is like a condition that society imposes upon the person who keeps it in return for being allowed to keep the animal.

Modern tort systems have extended the range of things for which there is strict liability. Some countries try to bring them under a general principle, not just to impose liability in odd cases such as dangerous animals. But not all countries have hit on the same principle.

In **France** there is strict liability for harm done by a thing under a person's control, whether a vehicle, stick, tree, or whatever. **German law** is less general. It lays down that the person in charge of a motor vehicle is strictly liable for bodily injury and property damage, as are those who run railways, electricity, gas, and some other enterprises. In other words, those who carry on the enterprises that make up the main sources of danger in an industrial society are strictly liable if harm results.

The **Anglo-American** approach has until recently been more limited. What are picked out for strict liability are specially danger-ous activities like using explosives. More recently the idea that a manufacturer is liable for defects in the goods he makes (**'products liability'**), even when he is not at fault, has begun to take hold. On this principle a company that makes a washing machine is liable to the buyer's wife if she is injured because of a fault in the machine. This is true even if the defect could not be discovered by careful inspection before the machine was sold.

The range of things for which there is strict liability is different in these systems of law. But on what underlying principle does it rest?

There seems to be some merit in the idea that, if in my own interest I have a thing under my control that can harm others, I should pay for the harm it causes. The fact that I **benefit**, or expect to benefit, and that I have **control**, justifies putting the risk that things will go wrong on me. The argument is especially powerful if I am in business and aim to make a profit from using the thing that does the harm. Paying compensation for the harm is then a business expense like any other.

But what of the opposing idea that, if I take care not to harm others, I should be free to act as I please? Why should I have to pay for accidents to other people that are not my fault? If they want to be compensated they should cover themselves by taking out insurance.

How does this apply to, say, a road accident caused by driving a vehicle? In French and German law the vehicle or driving counts as something for which the owner or driver is strictly liable if it causes an accident. In most systems based on the English common law the driver is liable only if he is at fault. But even these systems make the owner or driver carry insurance so that, **if he is at fault and harms someone**, the victim can recover from the owner or driver's insurance company.

So the difference between strict liability and fault liability for traffic accidents comes to this. Is the plaintiff in effect insured against harm caused by the defendant driver's fault (fault liability), or is he also insured against harm caused by the vehicle even without fault (strict liability)?

Which should we prefer? When drivers are liable only for fault, this may encourage them to be careful, if only to keep their insurance premiums down. On the other hand **people do recognize some responsibility for the harm they do even when they are not at fault**. If I run you down I should, morally speaking, stop and get help, even supposing that the accident was entirely your fault. If, then, I have some responsibility for the harm I do even when I am not at fault, and the insurance premium is not too heavy, there is a case for making me strictly liable for any accident my driving causes. To do this will make the victims of road accidents more secure, and so further one of the objects of the law. But it may also put up the cost of insurance.

Strict liability for people

So far we have discussed strict liability for things, or activities such as driving. Can there also be strict liability for other people? Is an **employer liable for the harm his employee causes** to someone while working for him? And is a parent responsible for harm done by his child who is under age? If the harm is more than trivial, it is not likely that the employee or child will be able to pay for it. So the chance of the victim being compensated depends on whether the employer or parent is liable.

Take first the case of employer's liability mentioned earlier. A labourer on a building site drops a brick on a passer-by and injures him. Does the builder, if he was not at fault in supervising his employee, have to compensate the passer-by for the injury? Legal systems give different answers. One is that the **builder must be at fault** as well as the labourer. The builder's fault might consist, for example, in taking on the labourer without proper inquiry or in not supervising his work. But often it is not easy to point to a fault of selection or supervision on the employer's part. In that case the plaintiff is not likely to receive compensation.

Another solution, more favourable to the plaintiff, is that the **employer** is liable only for fault but that, to escape liability, he **must prove that he was not at fault**. In other words, fault is presumed. In practice this makes it much easier for the plaintiff to get compensation. If it is not clear whether the employer was at fault or not, he will have to pay up.

A third solution, still more favourable to the plaintiff, is that if the employee is at fault the **employer is strictly liable for the employ-**

ee's fault. For the builder to be liable, however, the building labourer must have been at fault in the first place. If the labourer dropped the brick because there was a sudden explosion nearby the employer is not liable for what he did.

The argument for this (partial) strict liability is rather like that for strict liability for things. The employer gets the benefit of the employee's work and hopes to make a profit from the business in which he is employing the worker. He runs the business and has control, among other things, over the way in which the employee works. In return he has to pay for the harm his employees do to others, at least if they are at fault.

The case for strict liability is **weaker where parents are concerned**. They do not benefit, at least not directly, from having children to look after. They are not trying to make a profit from them. If a child does damage, for example by smashing the neighbour's window, in most countries parents are liable only if they were at fault in supervising their children. Some countries, however, assume that the parents were at fault and force them to prove that they were not, if they want to avoid paying compensation.

Apart from the law, if your child throws stones and breaks your neighbour's window, you would probably feel that you ought to pay for the damage, even if you did your best to stop your child throwing stones. This suggests that it is sometimes (morally) wrong not to pay for damage though the damage was not your fault.

One final point about strict liability. If compensation does not depend on proving that anyone was at fault, should we abandon tort law as an old-fashioned way of compensating injured people? Should we replace it, at least for accidental bodily injuries, by a **state-run insurance scheme**? Some people favour this, and some countries such as New Zealand have adopted a scheme of this sort.

It would be a radical (and perhaps expensive) step to make people pay compensation when they are not at fault and do not even control the person or thing that causes the harm.

Do we always have to be caring?

Some businesses advertise their services with slogans like 'Sameday Delivery Cares'. The obvious comment is that it would be a poor look-out if they didn't. But do we have to take care to avoid harm to others all the time, in every situation? Doesn't even the Good Samaritan need time off?

If you see a car with a flat tyre or an oil leak are you legally bound to tell the owner in case he does not notice the problem and has an accident as a result? It would certainly be a kindness to tell him. But if you don't, are you in a legal sense at fault?

All systems of law admit **some cases in which we are not bound to see that others are not injured**, though we could do so. Different systems express this idea in different ways. They may say that at times we have no duty to take care that others do not suffer harm. Or that it is sometimes lawful not to take care. Or that not taking care does not amount to fault. However expressed, the idea is that there are some risks of harm that those who suffer it ought to bear for themselves and not pass on to others.

Thus, people such as burglars have to take their chance of being injured while on the job. I need not see to it that a burglar who climbs on the roof to get into my house does not hurt himself because the tiles are loose. There is no reason why I should make things easier for him.

A more general point is that we do not have to be constantly on the look-out to do favours to strangers. Basically all of us should look after our own bodies and our own property. Take the case of seeing a stranger's car with a flat tyre or an oil leak. Or noticing that a suspicious character is lurking about your neighbour's property. It may be mean not to give a warning, but, if I do not, should that make me liable for the accident or theft that could probably have been prevented if I had given the warning?

Surely not. **But emergencies** may be an exception. Should the law (to take the standard example) allow me to stand by and let a child drown when I could rescue her without trouble? Should it allow a doctor to refuse to attend to an accident when asked to do so? Systems of tort and criminal law vary in what they say about our duty to try to **rescue a stranger from imminent danger**. (Obviously a parent or child-minder must take steps to save a child in his care and a doctor to save his own patient).

In some countries there is no duty to intervene to save a stranger. In others there is, and the plaintiff who suffers as a result can claim compensation from the person who failed to rescue her. In many European states it is actually a crime not to help in an emergency.

But the law nowhere forces me to risk my life or safety to protect a stranger. I do not have to intervene to stop a fight when to do that would put me at risk. Heroism, or 'having a go', is not compulsory.

These are some of the situations in which people who suffer harm cannot claim compensation from others who might have intervened to help them. In certain matters, we have to rely on ourselves, and not expect others to look after our interests. But where exactly should the line be drawn?

WHAT INTERESTS DOES TORT LAW PROTECT?

No system of tort law confines itself to giving compensation for bodily injuries and damage to property. Tort law ranges more widely and protects **other interests**, economic and personal. Here are two examples: the interest of a wife in being supported by her husband; and her interest in not suffering emotional distress through losing her husband (it can of course be the other way round).

Economic security

The first of these is an **economic**, the second an **emotional** interest. They both concern knock-on effects. Someone is killed by a tort and this in turn causes economic or emotional harm to their spouse and dependants. Should the law of torts treat these interests in economic and emotional security as rights for which compensation has to be paid?

If someone is killed by a tort (let us say run over by the defendant's negligent driving) their dependants **suffer economically**. The bread-winner has disappeared. The dead person is not there to claim what he would have earned had he lived, either from his employer or from the defendant. Should anyone have the right to claim from the defendant money that was never in fact earned?

Well, what about the breadwinner's wife? Should she be able to sue the defendant for the support that she would have received from the breadwinner had he lived? The same problem is raised as regards his children and close relatives whom he was supporting.

Some legal systems are **cautious about protecting purely economic interests**. If I am killed by your negligence it is not only my wife and family that suffer. So does my business partner, the shop where I bought my clothes, the charities to which I made regular gifts and so on. If these can all sue you, will there not be too many claims, some of them hard to check?

But should not my wife and close relatives at least be allowed to sue for loss of support? In many legal systems some relatives (spouses, children under age and often parents) have a **legal right to be supported**. So if you are responsible for my death, should they be allowed to claim support from you instead of me — at least to the extent that I actually was supporting them?

Even if they did not have a legal right to be supported, but I was **in fact supporting them**, have they not been deprived of something which they were entitled to think would continue? And does this also apply to the survivor of a couple who were living together without being married?

At one time most legal systems did not allow dependants to claim compensation for the death of a breadwinner. With the increase in accidental deaths in industrial society this had to change. Some countries now allow dependants to sue for loss of support if they had a legal right to be supported by the person killed and were actually receiving support. Others simply list the relatives who may claim if they were receiving support from the person killed.

Other countries again do not confine the claim for compensation to close relatives. They see **no reason why anyone who suffers economic loss** as a result of the death **should not have the right to claim compensation** from the person responsible. So an employer can sue someone who negligently kills a valuable employee, causing a loss to the business. A football club can sue the person responsible for killing its star footballer.

Emotional security

If a wife (and other dependants) can sue for loss of support when the breadwinner is killed by a tort, can they also claim to be compensated for the distress that the death causes them?

Legal systems tend to be **cautious about compensating for emotional distress**. One reason is that, while economic loss can be measured, it is almost impossible to gauge the extent of, say, a widow's bereavement. Indeed it is an intrusion on her privacy to try to assess it.

So some countries do not allow claims for bereavement at all. They think of bereavement as something we should bear ourselves. We should not try to convert it into money. Others allow a limited, nominal sum to be claimed: a few hundred pounds at most. This sidesteps the difficulty of trying to assess the actual distress caused by death. Some countries confine the claim, when they allow it, to spouses and close relatives. Others allow friends also to claim compensation if they have suffered serious distress.

But is emotional security something that the law can sensibly try to protect?

8
Forms and procedures

A procedure is a step, or series of steps, that must be taken if a certain result is to be achieved. A form is a device to record the steps taken, or the result achieved.

The sort of result that matters in law is whether something done is **legally valid** and so affects people's rights and duties. The 'something' may be a statute, treaty, contract, will, marriage etc. As a shorthand term, let us call these doings that are meant to affect rights and duties 'legal arrangements'. If a legal arrangement is valid it has legal effects. It may impose duties on the citizens, states, parties to the contract, spouses etc. or confer rights on them.

But a legal arrangement may be **invalid** because the correct procedure has not been followed. In that case citizens do not have to obey the statute. The parties do not have to carry out the contract. The would-be spouses are not husband and wife. The property of the dead person does not have to be given to the heir he appointed.

A legal arrangement can also be invalid because of its content. That means that, though the right procedure has been followed, the rights or duties it tried to create are not of the sort that the law allows.

A legal arrangement can be invalid because the law does not allow that sort of statute, contract, marriage, or will. A statute that provides for imprisonment without trial may be against the constitution. The law will refuse to enforce a contract by which Susan agrees never to work for anyone except Bob. It will treat a ceremony of marriage between John and Mary as void if they are brother and sister. If Susan makes a will leaving her property to whoever kills Alan, the law denies Alan's killer the right to claim the inheritance.

One might think that, in contrast with **content**, requirements of **form and procedure** are not important. That would be a mistake. Forms and procedures are important for a number of reasons. They make for certainty, they encourage careful reflection, and they promote fairness.

When a legal arrangement affects people's rights and duties, it is important to be **certain** exactly what rights and duties are created. Forms and procedures also help to make sure that legal arrangements take place only after **careful consideration**. There must be time to think before deciding. The arguments for and against need to be thrashed out. Lastly, procedures promote **fairness**; they are used to make sure that the parties to a dispute stand as far as possible on an even footing.

There is obviously some overlap between these various objects. All three are worth pursuing, but we have to ask whether in pursuing them law has become too formal. Has it become obsessed with seeing that the right procedure is followed rather than that the right result is reached?

Some think that formal and procedural safeguards should be multiplied; others that they should be kept to a minimum. The conflict is a bit like that between the supporters of the trustful and sceptical views of government (see Chapter 3).

REASONS FOR HAVING FORMS AND PROCEDURES

Certainty

The most obvious use of forms is to achieve certainty by recording that certain steps have been taken or certain acts done. Writing is important for this purpose. When we need to be sure of the exact terms of the legal arrangement, we usually insist that it should be in writing, or a least that there should be a written record of it. Statutes and treaties are always in writing. Contracts are put into writing if the parties want to be sure that there is no mistake about what has been agreed.

The law of **wills** offers a good example of the value of forms. When someone dies society has to decide who is to inherit his property. All systems of law allow a person who has died to leave at least part of his property as he wishes. But how can we be sure who he wanted to leave it to?

It would be rash to rely on what his relatives and friends say about his wishes after he is dead. They may falsify what he said in their own interest, or may not remember it correctly. Even if they tell the truth, and their memory is accurate, the person who has died may have changed his mind since he spoke to them. Being secretive or not wanting to stir up jealousy, he may not have told anyone that he wanted his property to go to Jane rather than Susan.

Hence systems of law are not satisfied with a statement by a relative or friend of what the person who has died said his wishes were. They demand more reliable evidence. Writing is essential. Some countries are satisfied with a dated letter in the handwriting of the person who has since died. Others require more: a written and dated document signed by him in the presence of witnesses, which he told them was his will, and which they too sign as witnesses.

Why go to this length? First, to ensure that the document that is produced when the person is no longer alive to explain himself **really is his will**. That is why, if witnesses are required, the person making his will has to tell the witnesses that the document is his will, though he does not have to tell them what is in it. Otherwise the document might be a draft, or a joke.

Secondly, the fact that the will has to be in writing makes sure that the wishes of the person who has died are on record in a form that, short of forgery, **cannot be altered after his death**. If he has expressed himself accurately his true wishes will then be put into effect. If he has not expressed properly what he had in mind, if he has mentioned Jane when he meant Susan, the law will, unless the mistake is obvious, not put his real wishes into effect.

This is because a written will is treated as a more reliable guide to what the dead person wanted than what other people now say he wanted. It is a text to be interpreted, not altered (see Chapter 9). That may seem harsh, but it is probably better than to allow his relatives or friends to contradict what is in the will. And if Jane is satisfied that the dead person really meant Susan, she can give Susan the money she inherits.

The reason why a will must be dated is that **only a person's last will counts**. He can change his mind up to the moment of his death. So the formalities for a will reflect the need for certainty and also give effect to certain policies: that a person may leave his property, or most of it, to anyone he pleases; that he may change his mind up to the last moment of his life; and that he need not tell anyone who he has decided to leave it to. A society that did not agree with these policies would have different formalities for wills, or might not allow wills at all.

Certainty, and hence form, can also be important to establish the **fact** of a legal arrangement. **Marriage** is an example. It is now nearly always a formal act, though in the past a man and woman got married simply by deciding to treat one another as husband and wife and live together permanently.

The formalities for marriage laid down in many modern systems of law are that the marriage must take place before a person authorised to conduct marriages, in a place set aside for the purpose, after public notice has been given of the couple's intention to marry. The marriage is then recorded in an official register, of which copies are available when needed.

The reason why marriage is now nearly always a formal act is not that the couple want to put on record who is to do the cooking or look after the children. Unlike a will, it is not the content of their agreement that they want to put on record. If they want that, they make a separate contract; but there is no need to do so, since the law already lays down the main duties and rights of husband and wife.

The point of making marriage formal is rather to establish beyond doubt that **the couple have the status of man and wife**. For that purpose a procedure is needed that cannot be misunderstood and that creates a permanent record of their agreement to take one another as husband and wife. The publicity is meant to ensure that only those who are entitled to marry get married — for instance (in a country where only one wife or husband is allowed at a time) that they are not married already.

The informal alternative

There is usually an informal alternative to these formal arrangements. A couple do not have to marry. They can choose to live together without getting married. To insist on marriage may show a want of trust in one's partner. Most contracts do not have to be in writing, though some legal systems insist on written evidence of a contract before they will enforce it (see Chapter 5). Even so, the parties to a contract, if they prefer, can rely on what has been verbally agreed. To insist on writing can look like a sign of mistrust.

Nor is anyone bound to leave a will. If I die without making one (intestate) it is up to my close relatives who then automatically inherit my property to decide what to do with it. I can, if I wish, tell them what I should **like** them to do and trust them to carry out my wishes. But, apart from some rare cases, law does not **make** them do what they have informally said they would.

Even a government often decides not to deal with a problem by putting forward legislation but tries instead to persuade people to act as it wants. **Informal persuasion,** if effective, **is better than compulsion.** If it turns out not to be effective, there is the threat that legislation will follow. If it does, it turns an informal moral or social duty into a formal, legal one.

If people can be persuaded not to pollute rivers without pollution being made a crime, so much the better. But if they cannot, the government may have to put forward legislation to impose penalties on those guilty of it.

Even if most people want to avoid polluting rivers, it may be better to prohibit pollution by law than to rely on persuasion. The advantage of a formal rule is that it strikes at the minority of people who don't care about, say, pollution. They take a free ride on the backs of those who do care about pollution and take trouble to avoid it.

A formal rule can also **tell people exactly what they are supposed to do.** It can define pollution and lay down the steps to avoid it. Unless this is done some people will not know what it is they should avoid, and how to set about it.

On the other hand legislation is expensive because it has to be enforced by inspectors and courts. Whether the enterprises concerned obey the law or not they pay extra in the form of increased costs or fines.

Careful consideration

Forms and procedures also serve to reduce the chance of hasty decisions that may ruin peoples' happiness. They remind us before we marry, make a will, or sign a written contract to look before we leap. The same is true of rules of procedure that make legislatures and other public bodies consider proposals more than once before they agree to them: hence for example the rule in many countries that proposed legislation must be considered ('read') three times before being passed.

Fairness

How can we try to ensure that disputes between citizens or between citizens and the state are fairly dealt with? In dealing with disputes, fairness and justice (see Chapter 10) require that the parties should be equal before the law. Equality before the law, if it is to be a reality, does not just mean that the same rules of law apply to all. Something more is called for. Each party to the dispute must have an equal chance to put their case. And the judge or official who decides the dispute must not be biased.

If dispute and trial procedure is to be fair, it is important that the community should value fairness. It is also vital that the police, judges, and officials should be honest and conscientious. But these virtues do not come automatically. What they imply needs to be spelled out and reinforced by law.

In many countries this is done by codes of criminal and private (sometimes also of administrative) procedure. These lay down rules for criminal investigations and trials; for private lawsuits; and for administrative decisions and complaints about them. Even when they do not have codes (see Chapter 2) most countries have detailed rules of procedure for dealing with disputes.

THE CITIZEN VERSUS THE STATE

We shall focus on one important question about procedure and fairness. **Is equality before the law possible** when the state is a party to the dispute? Can the citizen suspected or charged with a crime be put on an equal footing with the state, with its vast resources? For the state in one capacity or another investigates, prosecutes, tries and punishes the suspected criminal.

Fairness is also difficult to achieve in administrative law, where the state has to put policies approved by the legislature into effect and at the same time to be fair to those affected by them. It has, for example, to build roads but at the same time to take account of the objections of people who will suffer if a road is built in this place rather than that.

But we shall concentrate here on criminal procedure.

Criminal procedure

The private citizen who is suspected or charged with a crime is in a very weak position compared with the state. He has nothing like the same resources at his disposal. He may be arrested and kept in custody while the crime is further investigated, so that he is hampered in collecting evidence with which to meet the charge. He does not have the physical strength to defend himself if the police beat him up.

To redress the balance the person suspected or charged with a crime can be protected in various ways. These vary from one legal system to another, but all systems now try to provide **some** safeguards.

One way of protecting the suspected criminal is by **dividing the stages in criminal procedure between different bodies**. One can separate the functions of investigating, prosecuting, trying, deciding guilt, sentencing and carrying out the sentence. Six or seven different bodies can each be given one of these jobs.

For example the police can be in charge of investigating the crime; a prosecution service of prosecuting; the judges of presiding over the trial; a jury of deciding whether to convict; an appeal court of settling whether the trial was fair; a prison service of carrying out the sentence if the suspect is convicted and sentenced to prison.

The judge who presides over the trial usually sentences the suspect if he is convicted, but even that is not inevitable. Sentencing can be entrusted to a special board. Or a judge can be put in charge of the investigation and a different judge chosen to try the case if the first judge finds there is enough evidence to justify a trial.

All these procedural devices remind us of the **separation of powers** that was discussed in Chapter 3. The idea is that no one authority (police, prosecution, judge, jury, prison service) should have too much power. State powers should be sliced up, and the slices should be able to keep a check on one another. The police will not be able to prosecute unless they can persuade the prosecution service that there is a strong case. The judge will if necessary rule at the trial that the prosecution has not produced enough evidence. If the jury think the judge has shown bias during the trial they will probably acquit the suspect even though they might otherwise have convicted him. If the suspect is convicted but thinks the procedure has been unfair he can appeal to a higher court. If all else fails the person convicted may be able to persuade the government to advise the head of state to pardon him or reduce the sentence.

In contrast with systems that divide up the various bits of the criminal process there are those that concentrate them. Some countries have a centralized system of prosecuting and trying crimes. The Minister of Justice controls the police and the investigation of crime. He appoints the judges who try criminal cases. The judges' promotion depends on him. There is no jury; judges decide on guilt or innocence without a jury.

Is the divided or the centralized system better? The divided system is more complicated, more expensive and probably results in more acquittals. On the other hand it is more likely to be seen as fair by the person tried and sentenced.

The jury

The jury differs from the other bodies concerned with criminal procedure. All the others are branches of the state. This is true even if the police are made up of local rather than national forces. They all represent public authority and are paid from public funds. **The jury,** however, is chosen from and **represents private citizens**. It brings a popular element into criminal justice.

In most common law countries (see Chapter 2) serious crimes are tried by judge and jury. The number of members of the jury varies but twelve is common. The judge explains to the jury the law to be applied, for instance what amounts to murder. The jury decide whether the suspect did what he is said to have done (say, shot his rival dead) and, if so, whether in the light of the law set out by the judge, he is guilty of murder. A jury decides either unanimously or by a majority, depending on the country where the trial takes place. It gives no reasons for its decision.

Many people think that trial by jury helps to redress the balance between the state and the suspect. If a case is tried by jury the state has to persuade all or the majority of a group of ordinary citizens that the suspect is guilty, not merely one or a few judges. Juries are on the whole conscientious in deciding the case according to the law explained to them by the judge. But they occasionally acquit some-one, even if they think that he committed the crime, because they consider that it was unfair to charge him with it.

Juries may however **share the prejudices of ordinary people** against unpopular groups. The fact that, unlike judges, they do not have to give reasons for their decision (in fact are not allowed to) makes it more difficult to criticise their verdict if there is an appeal against it. Sometimes, then, trial by a judge or judges can be fairer.

What other ways are there of redressing the balance between the suspected criminal and the state, so that they are more or less equal before the law?

There are many possibilities. It is important that the person charged should **know the evidence against him** as soon as possible and should have access to legal advice and, if the charge is serious, the help of a trained advocate. In some countries the prosecution on a criminal charge has to disclose its evidence in advance but the defence does not have to do the same until the trial. In that case the parties are not on an equal footing **so far as disclosure is concerned**. But this, and similar devices, can be seen as part of an attempt to reduce the advantage that the prosecution has because of its greater resources.

Some countries have a rule that a suspect cannot be forced to answer questions put by the police, because his answers might point to his guilt. He is **not bound to incriminate himself**. Nor can he be questioned at the trial unless he chooses to give evidence. The prosecutor and judge cannot comment on the fact that he does not choose to explain his behaviour.

In other countries a suspect **can be forced to answer questions** when arrested, since if he does not this will tell against him at the trial. The trial itself begins with a series of questions put to the suspect by the judge. In many civil law systems (see Chapter 2) the judge thinks of himself as trying to discover the truth, rather than as refereeing a contest between the prosecution and the defence.

The difference between these methods of trying suspects is partly a matter of history and tradition. In common law countries the judge in a criminal trial is more like a referee; in civil law countries more like an investigator. But in all countries the detailed rules vary according to the degree to which it is thought necessary to protect the suspect against the superior power of the state.

The presumption of innocence

An important way of redressing the balance between the suspect and the state is the so-called '**presumption of innocence**'. Despite its name, this does not mean that if someone is arrested and charged with a crime he is generally thought to be innocent. On the contrary, **most people**, outside a law-court, will **assume that he is guilty**. To counteract this general assumption, it is everywhere a rule of criminal procedure that **the state** or prosecutor **must prove the suspect's guilt**. If the state does not succeed in doing this, the judge or jury hearing the case are bound to acquit him. To be acquitted, the suspect does not have to show that he is innocent.

The effect of this rule is that, if the evidence leaves a serious doubt as to the guilt of the person charged he is acquitted. He gets the benefit of the doubt.

Some people think that the effort to be fair to those suspected of crimes is made at the expense of the effectiveness of the criminal law in keeping deviant behaviour within bounds. That may be so, but fairness may have other, more healthy consequences. It may be that, **the more fairly criminal trials are conducted, the greater the attachment of ordinary people to the rule of law.**

9
Interpretation

Interpretation is one of the main concerns of lawyers.

Originally, lawyers were people who specialized in drafting and interpreting documents, rather than arguing cases in court or judging disputes. A person drafting a document must try to see in advance how the law, treaty, contract or will he is drafting will be interpreted, so that his text covers the areas he wants it to cover. Arguments in court are often about the interpretation of a text, and judges have to decide what the right interpretation is. So, one way and another, **interpretation is a key part of legal practice**.

How documents should be interpreted is disputed. Suppose a by-law forbids vehicles in a park. Does this apply to bicycles, motor-cycles or powered lawn-mowers? More important, how do you set about deciding? Do you go by the dictionary meaning of the word 'vehicle'? Do you ask what purpose banning vehicles from the park is meant to serve? Do you ask what hardship to the public would be caused if, for example, bicycles or baby-carriages were included in the ban? Or how inconvenient it would be if powered lawn-mowers were excluded?

Some lawyers give priority to the **letter of the text**, others to its **spirit or purpose**, others again to the likely result of interpreting it this way or that. This chapter is mainly concerned with the clash between these different approaches.

WHAT IS INTERPRETATION?

First of all, what is interpretation? To interpret what someone says is to attach a meaning to their remarks. When the meaning is at once clear the remark does not have to be interpreted, but if it is not clear, or not immediately clear, it does. The interpreter then has to choose between two or more possible ways of understanding what was said.

Wanting to travel to Manchester, you ask me to get you a time-table. I am not sure whether you meant a coach time-table or a railway time-table. I may be able to ask you which you meant. But if I cannot, I have to make up my mind, perhaps on the basis of how you usually travel, or what the easiest way of getting to Manchester is.

Interpreting a request of this sort is not just interpreting the words 'please get me a time-table', which are straightforward enough, but interpreting them in the context of a purpose, a wish to travel to Manchester. Interpreting texts, which is so central a part of a lawyer's work, is in some ways similar. A lawyer interprets a text as part of a statute, contract, will, treaty, regulation or whatever. But there are differences. When I have to interpret your request for a time-table I am free to go about it in any way I choose. A lawyer's interpretation of a text is a more formal process.

Legal interpretation is formal

It is formal, first, because the texts a lawyer interprets are **in writing**. Not only are they in writing but they have authority. If they are statutes they are part of state law. If they are contracts or treaties they bind the parties to the contract or treaty. If they are wills they bind whoever is dealing with the property of the person who has died. The interpretation chosen will make a difference to someone's rights and duties.

There is another way in which the interpretation of a legal text is formal. When it is disputed, there is such a thing as an **official interpretation** of the text. Judges provide this when they try cases or hear appeals. Ministers and civil servants, for example tax officials, also issue official interpretations of statutes, though their interpretations have in the end to give way to those of judges if there is a difference of opinion between the two.

Another way in which the interpretation of legal texts is unlike interpreting a request from a friend is that the evidence on which the interpreter of legal texts has to come to a decision is limited. If I am not sure what my friend meant by his request my best move is to ask him. But the **interpreter of a legal text cannot solve the problem by going back to the author of the text** and asking what he meant. For one thing, legal texts often have no single author. They are enacted by legislators, hundreds in number, or agreed by the parties to a contract or treaty, of whom there may be many.

Legislators do not have time to explain what they meant by the statutes they have passed. Even if they did, and all agreed, it might not be a good idea to ask them, because they would be tempted to explain the law with the benefit of hindsight. They would be tempted to put themselves in a better light by saying that it meant something that they would not have said it meant at the time it was passed. This would not be fair to those who have to obey the law. They are entitled to be judged by what in the view of an impartial person the law meant at the time they had to obey it.

The interpreter of a **will** obviously cannot consult the testator about what it meant, as he is dead. It might seem that the interpreter of a **contract** or **treaty** could consult the parties to the treaty or contract. But if a dispute has arisen it is often because the parties disagree about how it should be interpreted. A neutral interpretation is called for. So to ask the parties is not a real option. In general, problems of interpreting legal texts cannot be solved by going back to the authors of the text.

Another way in which the evidence available to the interpreter of a text is limited is that **the text has to speak for itself**. Earlier drafts of a statute, will, contract or treaty are superseded by the final version. The authors of the text are committed to the final version, and this replaces whatever discussions or negotiations went on beforehand. Even what the authors said they meant at the time the text was agreed is treated with reserve. For instance, some systems of law do not accept that in interpreting the text of a statute the interpreter can go by what the Minister said it meant when he spoke in the legislature.

How far one presses the idea that a text should speak for itself is a matter of dispute, but at its core there lies a sound idea. This is that a person who agrees that a certain form of words is to be binding should be willing for the words to be taken in their ordinary sense. Otherwise he should have insisted on a different form of words or said at the time that he attached a **special meaning** to them, not the ordinary meaning.

Attaching a special meaning is in fact quite a common practice. Statutes and contracts often have clauses that lay down the meaning to be given to the words they use. For instance they may say that 'owner' includes the occupier of a house. In that case a tenant who does not own the house is treated for purposes of the statute (but not otherwise) as if he did. Behind this practice lies the view that in legal texts the words should be taken in their ordinary sense unless the author of the text lays down a different sense.

WHAT IS THE BEST APPROACH TO INTERPRETATION?

The textual approach

The idea that a text must speak for itself embodies one approach to interpretation, which I shall call the textual approach. It holds that a text must be understood in its **ordinary sense**. If vehicles are excluded from the park that means that what are ordinarily spoken of as vehicles (cars, coaches, trucks) are excluded. This may be inconvenient if it means, for example, that some disabled people cannot use the park because they can only get there by a motorized vehicle. But that has to be accepted.

Sometimes of course a word or phrase has no ordinary sense, because it is not one used by ordinary people. When technical terms, legal or scientific, are used, what corresponds to the ordinary meaning of the term is its technical meaning. The technical meaning is what it ordinarily means to legal or scientific experts.

But those who favour the textual approach admit that there are exceptional cases where it is unsatisfactory. When it would produce an **absurd result** to read the words in their ordinary sense, they can be interpreted in a different sense, one that does not produce an absurd result.

What amounts to an absurd result is of course debatable; what is absurd to one judge is merely unusual to another. Would it be absurd if the meaning given to 'vehicle' resulted in excluding some disabled people from the park? A text that is self-contradictory or unworkable in practice is clearly absurd, but how far one should treat a meaning that some people think unreasonable as absurd is not clear.

However we understand absurdity, the textual approach gives priority to the language used in the text in its ordinary sense over other evidence of the author's intention. The textual approach is sometimes attacked by critics, who call it '**literalism**', going by the letter. But what is the point of putting a statute, contract, treaty, or will into words unless those words are to be treated as binding?

The purposive approach

A different approach to interpreting texts is the purposive approach. According to this, priority in interpreting texts should be given to the **purpose** of the statute, contract, treaty, will, or regulation. Account should also be taken of the **general aims of the legal system**, such as justice, security, and efficiency. This is specially important in interpreting statutes. A law (say the law forbidding vehicles in the park) can have special purposes of its own (say to ensure peace and quiet for those who use the park). But more general purposes have also to be taken into account (for instance that public places should be kept tidy, which may require powered lawn-mowers to be admitted even if they make a noise).

If these special or general purposes point to an interpretation different from the ordinary meaning of the words, supporters of the purposive approach say that the 'purposive' meaning should be adopted in preference to the ordinary meaning.

In looking for the purpose of a document there are, however, some limits on how far afield one can range. Legal systems vary a bit in the limits they set. When a statute is interpreted the interpreter can certainly look at the whole statute and any earlier laws on the subject. He can take account of what the previous state of the law was and what were thought to be its defects. Supporters of the purposive approach go further, and say that the interpreter should be able to take account of reports and proposals of official commissions and other materials prepared with a view to passing a law or making a treaty. Many systems of law do in fact allow these materials to be considered.

A ' drinking and driving' example

Which approach is better, the textual or the purposive approach? I take an example (altering it a bit) from a law in Britain that has since been replaced. Suppose a statute lays down that a policeman may require someone who is driving a vehicle to take a blood test. If the blood test shows that he has more than a certain amount of alcohol in the blood, he may be charged with the offence of drinking and driving.

What does 'driving' mean in this statute? Like most words, 'driving' has a range of meanings. But in its ordinary meaning, many people would say, a person is driving a vehicle when he is at the controls and the vehicle is moving. When the vehicle stops he stops driving. But if we interpret driving in this way, we make the statute absurd. How could a policeman tell a driver to take a blood test while the vehicle was moving?

So, even on the textual approach, we ought to ask if 'driving' can be understood in another way. If the statute is to have some point, the driver must still be driving after he has stopped the vehicle because the policeman has told him to. Can driving be understood in this wider sense? It probably can, since from one point of view the driver of a vehicle is driving from the moment he sets off until he gets to his destination, even if he stops on the way for a meal. If asked during the meal what he was doing he would say he was 'driving to Manchester'. So does 'driving' in the statute mean simply that the driver is still on the way to his destination?

From the words alone this is a possible interpretation. But ought not the purpose of the law to be taken into account when we interpret 'driving'? The point of the law is surely to make the person driving liable to take a blood test; and the purpose of this is to reduce the danger that the motorist will drive with more than a certain amount of alcohol in his blood. Would it fit that purpose to give a blood test to someone having a meal who has not been driving for the last half-hour and may not set off again for some time? Would it be fair to him?

Perhaps, taking the purpose of the law into account, a driver is 'driving' only if he has already started and means to go on with the journey the moment he can. It is only then that, if the alcohol in his blood is over the limit, he will be a danger on the road. In that case he may be driving though he is temporarily at a halt in a traffic jam, or because a policeman has stopped him. If the driver has stopped for a meal he is not driving for the purpose of the blood test, but the driver who has got out of his car in a traffic jam to buy a paper is still driving.

On the textual approach the ordinary meaning of 'driving' (that the vehicle must be in motion) leads to an absurdity, so that other ways of understanding 'driving' can be considered. On the purposive approach the ordinary meaning of 'driving' has no special priority and a motorist can be said to be driving when it would promote the purpose of the drinking and driving law to give him a blood test. This might suggest a very wide interpretation of driving, one that would include the stage when he is having a meal on the way.

But the purpose of reducing drinking and driving is not the only purpose that the interpreter has to take into account. There are also general aims of the legal system. One of these is to be fair to people who may be charged with a crime. They should be able to know roughly when they are in danger of being tested and prosecuted. This brings us back by a roundabout route to the ordinary meaning of 'driving'. When a statute uses a term that is part of ordinary language, those affected by it are likely to understand it in its ordinary sense. So the purposes of the legal system itself require close attention to be paid to the words used in the text.

Words cannot mean just anything

Though words have a range of meanings, they cannot mean just anything. For instance, there are some things that 'driving' could not mean. A driver whose vehicle is in the garage and who has not yet set off, though he intends to leave shortly, and who is in the meantime having a few drinks, is not driving. It is true that, if he were held to be driving, the purpose of the law against drinking and driving would be satisfied. But this cannot justify the interpreter in stretching the meaning of driving to cover the driver whose vehicle is still in the garage.

It is very rare for a judge to decide that a text **means something that it could not mean in ordinary or technical language**. On the few occasions when a judge does this, he does it because he thinks that an obvious mistake has been made by the author of the text, and that he has a duty to correct it.

There is little doubt that 'or' cannot mean 'and'. **Elephants and hyenas** means both species, but **elephants or hyenas** means one of the two. So if a statute lays down that no one may hunt elephants and hyenas without a licence, the draftsman has probably made a mistake. As it stands, the law seems to say that one may hunt either elephants or hyenas without a licence but not both. It is unlikely that this is what the legislators meant. Most hunters will be hunting one or the other, not both, and the prohibition will then have very little effect.

So if a judge had to interpret this statute he would probably interpret 'and' as 'or', and say that 'elephants and hyenas' should read as if it said 'elephants or hyenas'. That seems to go against the textual approach, by taking a word to mean what it cannot mean. It seems as if the judge is opting for the purposive approach, in order to make the statute workable. A different way of putting it, more consistent with the textual approach, is that the judge has the power to correct an obvious mistake by substituting 'or' for 'and'. In that case he is not interpreting the text but correcting it, something that can obviously be allowed only within very narrow limits.

Intention

The textual approach and the purposive approach are often put forward as different ways of getting at the **intention of the author of the text**. That is not quite right, because the textual approach opts for what the words ordinarily mean, and the author of the text may not have meant to use the actual words he did (take the elephants and hyenas example).

But assuming the author of the text did mean to use the words he used, there is sometimes a contrast between what he meant by the words used and what he meant to achieve by using them. These are two different things, though they can both be called his 'intention'. Does it help to think of interpretation as a search for the intention of the legislators, the parties to the contract etc?

Individuals have both sorts of intention, and bodies like legislatures and associations can have both too. But often the members of these bodies do not study the texts that are produced in their name at all carefully. They can say roughly what they want to achieve by passing a law. They may for example be against drinking and driving and in favour of animal conservation. But they probably have not thought about what is meant by 'driving' in the blood testing statute or 'elephants and hyenas' in the hunting statute.

All the same there is good reason, I think, to say that the interpreter should try to discover the intention of the legislature or the parties to a contract or treaty. A statute, contract or treaty is a **compromise between different views**. Perhaps no member of the legislature, and no party to the contract or treaty, would themselves have chosen the text that was finally agreed, if it depended on them alone. The point of speaking of the intention of the legislature or the contracting parties is not that any particular person's views should govern the interpretation of the text. It is rather that the interpreter should treat the text **as if it represented the views of a single individual**, and make it as coherent as the words permit.

This is a fiction, but it expresses a sound policy. The interpreter should not treat the views of individual members of a large body as if they were the views of the whole body. There may have been no agreed view about what the text meant. In the same way, the views of one party to a contract about what the contract means should be not be treated as if they were the views of both parties. The interpreter should aim at a neutral, impartial reading of the text and its purposes.

Whether the textual or the purposive approach to interpretation is preferred, every text has to be seen against the background of the society and the legal system of which it forms part.

10

Justice

Governments are expected to have many virtues. They should be efficient, expand the economy, and defend the national interest. The legal system, as part of government, should work smoothly.

But, more important, it is expected to be **just**. People think that laws should be just and should be administered in a just, fair, equitable way. These three words — just, fair, equitable — describe much the same ideal. The administration of law is called the administration of justice and the person who runs it is in many countries the Minister of Justice. Admittedly there are unjust laws, but many people see these as aberrations, not proper laws.

But how **can laws be just**? And, supposing they were just, **how could they be justly administered**? For we don't agree about what justice is. Compare justice with health. We know what it is to be healthy and can see, at least in outline, what sort of medical service would make us healthier. But we don't agree about what a just society would be like, or what laws there would be in a just society.

Would people be equally well off in a just society? Or would there be inequalities based on differences in talent, upbringing, efforts and opportunity? To argue about equality is the stuff of politics, of the conflict between right and left, and no agreement about it is in sight. Should we then throw in the sponge? Should we say that the so-called just society is simply a name for the society that you or I would prefer to live in?

Though I do not agree with it, this sceptical view has some attraction when we ask what a just society would be like. But if we think about what it is for a law to be unjust, or to be unfairly administered, we can arrive, I think, at a reasonable measure of agreement. We can agree enough to make it unlikely that a law's being unjust or unfairly administered is merely a matter of personal preference.

In other words, **justice is at least partly objective**. If so, it is worth asking what makes laws and their administration just, and what stops them being unjust.

UNJUST LAWS

Laws give people rights and impose duties on them. In this way they distribute benefits and burdens among citizens. Whether the laws are just depends on whether rights and duties are allotted fairly.

Often laws give the same rights and impose the same duties on everybody. No one is entitled to steal. Every child is entitled to free education. But they do not always do this. When laws do not treat everyone equally, we must ask **whether there is a good reason for discriminating**. Suppose that the vote is given to men and not women, or that men but not women are liable to military service. Is it fair to make a distinction between the sexes as regards voting or military service?

These examples bring out a central point about justice. A law can be criticised not only for discriminating when there should be no discrimination but also for **not discriminating when there should be discrimination**. A law that imposes military service equally on both sexes (especially if women are expected to fight) is open to criticism for **not** drawing a distinction between the sexes.

The background to our thinking about discrimination seems to be this. Rights should be given and duties imposed on all alike, unless there is a good reason why in a particular case they should not. We all have a **roughly equal capacity to enjoy life, liberty and happiness** and to help others enjoy these good things. So we should be treated as equally responsible beings, entitled to rights and subject to duties. But the equality is only rough, and does not apply to every area of life.

If this way of thinking about justice is on the right lines, the main problem about just laws is: which differences between people should count in allotting rights and duties? Which should be disregarded?

Allotting rights

Rights give people benefits and opportunities they might not otherwise have. But on what basis should the state allot rights? Various reasons are put forward for giving benefits to some rather than others, or more benefits to some than to others. On one view priority should go to those who are **abler**, or have **achieved more**, or have greater **needs** or **responsibilities**. Their contribution or burdens are greater than the average. So they deserve extra consideration or need extra help. On the other hand supporters of equality argue that for the state to deny a person something that is given to others, unless there is a good reason for denying it, is to deny them the respect that is their due.

It seems to follow that some laws that distribute rights are unjust, because they give something equally when they should make a distinction, or make a distinction when they should not. But much depends on the sort of right involved. Take **the right to vote**. This is something that most people want. It gives them a say in deciding who is to govern them.

Should everyone have the vote? In practice **children** below a certain age are denied it, on the ground that they are less able to make a sensible choice and have fewer responsibilities than adults. The same reasons used to be given for not giving **women** the vote, and in some countries for not giving it to **black people**. In most countries **foreigners** and **prisoners** still cannot vote.

Why should this be? Obviously opinions have changed about whether women can make sensible choices. But equally important has been the thought that people need the vote to protect their interests. The responsibilities of women are as heavy as those of men, or heavier. But foreigners do not need the vote so much, for they can generally vote in their own countries. The argument against giving prisoners the vote is that they have shown that they do not respect the values of the community that are embodied in its laws. On the other hand they need the vote to protect their interests as much as anyone.

If we assume that voting laws in modern democracies are not unjust, there must be cases in which it is just to give a right to all the members of a group (women, ethnic minorities) and cases in which it is permissible not to give it to any of them (the young, foreigners, prisoners). Several factors have to be taken into account in making a just voting law: the respect owed to all, but also people's varying needs and capacities. And if this true of the vote it may be true of other rights as well.

It does not follow that when these factors are taken into account there is **only one just way of deciding who can vote**. A country that gives resident foreigners or prisoners the vote is not acting unjustly, though it would not be unjust to refuse it either. In that case there is no uniquely just way of giving and refusing the right to vote, but we can point to some that are unjust and others that are not.

It is quite easy to point to factors that could not properly be taken into account in deciding who can vote. It would not be fair to make **a person's height or surname** a factor in deciding who could vote, because it is not true that people of a certain height or surname are more capable or need the vote more than others.

Yet height can rightly be taken into account in other contexts. People above a certain height may be better qualified for the police force than others because height inspires respect. People of a certain ethnic or religious group may need to be protected against discrimination more than others, because there is a strong prejudice against that group. Justice does not require every right to be made available on exactly the same basis. When rights are allotted and the justice of the allocation is disputed, it makes a difference what the point of giving people the right is.

Allotting duties and burdens

Much the same is true when burdens are imposed. On what basis is it just to **impose taxes**? Should they fall on all citizens **equally**, like a poll tax? Or should the amount of tax depend on **ability to pay**? Should it depend on the **benefit** that the tax-payer gets from the thing taxed? Or on the taxpayer's **responsibilities**?

These factors are the other side of the coin from those we met in connection with rights. Benefit corresponds to need, ability to pay, achievement and so on. And there is the more general point that the state should aim at a balance between rights and duties, benefits and burdens, so that those who benefit more from the laws it makes can justly have heavier burdens imposed on them.

How exactly we should weigh these factors in arriving at a just system of taxation is not easy to say. But a just system of income tax would probably take account of **ability** to pay, the **responsibilities** of the tax-payer, and the **benefits** he derives from the legal framework in which he can earn his living.

There are several ways of combining these factors that are not unjust. On the other hand it is easy to point to schemes that **would be unjust**. It would be unjust to replace income tax by a poll tax that was the same for everyone. This would disregard the taxpayer's

unjust. Unjust laws are awkward not only for ordinary people who have to decide whether to obey them but also for judges and officials who have to decide whether to apply them. For **to apply an unjust law strictly and impartially is to spread injustice**.

Suppose a government replaces the income tax by a poll tax, so that, though incomes vary widely, everyone pays the same. The poll tax would be widely regarded as unjust, and with good reason. It is fair to tax people the same when the benefit they get, or can get, from the thing taxed is roughly the same. So it may be fair to make every owner or hirer of a TV set pay the same fee for a licence to use it, even though some rarely watch TV and others are glued to the set.

But income tax is a contribution to the general expense of running a society. It is not a tax on a particular item. The highly paid are much better placed to contribute to these general expenses than the low paid. They also get more benefit from the legal system, since, without the framework of law and the security it provides, they could earn little or nothing.

Supposing, then, that income tax was replaced by a poll tax, ought officials and judges to apply it impartially, taking no account of high or low income? Opinions differ. One view is that **judges and officials should apply even unjust laws impartially**. They are professionally committed to applying the law as it is, even if it is unjust. Their remedy, if the laws as a whole are too unjust, is to resign their office. Others think that it is **sometimes right for them to stay on as judges and try to undermine the system**.

Consider the parallel with doctors. A doctor should try to heal even a mass murderer, though society would be better off if he died. We rely on doctors to promote life and health. We do not think they should weigh up whether in a particular case the patient is so wicked that he doesn't deserve to live. In much the same way we rely on judges to apply the laws and not to ask themselves whether a particular law would be better not applied. But they can, like the rest of us, criticize it, and, if it offends their conscience, resign.

It is a different question whether a citizen is bound to obey an unjust law. In general we have, I believe, a duty to obey the law, assuming that it offers us a reasonable balance of duties and rights, threats and promises. But if a law is unjust we may not have a duty to obey it. Sometimes there is, morally speaking, a choice. If income tax were replaced by a poll tax, it would not be wrong to disobey it, but also not wrong to pay the tax. That the tax is unjust is a reason not to pay it, but the fact that if I do not pay the unjust tax I do not contribute to the expense of the society to which I belong is a reason for paying it. We have to choose between two options, each morally permissible, taking into account that we may suffer a sanction if we break the law.

But some laws are so oppressive that one ought positively not to obey them. If a law was passed that required parents to inform the police if their children took drugs, it would be wrong to obey it, since that would be to disrupt family life.

Equity

It is another matter **whether a judge should apply a law, just or unjust, strictly**. Laws have to be framed in general terms. These are often not well adapted to particular cases, and no two cases are exactly alike. In the nature of things laws cannot fit perfectly, because situations arise that were not, and could not have been, foreseen by those who made them. All systems of law take account of this. They give judges some power to make exceptions when it seems fair to do so. The extent of the power varies from country to country and from one branch of the law to another, but it always exists.

The exercise of this power is often called **equity**. If income tax was replaced by a poll tax, courts would try to find ways of protecting those who suffered special hardship from having to pay the tax. They have done this, and continue to do it, in a striking way in the law of contracts (see Chapter 5).

People should, generally speaking, keep their promises and perform their contracts. But it can be unfair to hold people to the contracts they have made. Someone who buys a washing machine may have been **pressurized** into buying it. Or the seller may have **misled** them about its performance. Courts have found ways of protecting buyers who agree to buy something through mistake or deception or undue pressure. One way is to allow the buyer to return the machine and get his money back. And judges are alive to other reasons why it is sometimes unfair to enforce a bargain, for instance when the **bargaining power** of the parties to the contract is **very unequal**.

Justice requires general rules to be modified to fit situations where they would otherwise cause serious hardship. But, here again, though it would clearly be unjust to take no account of the pressures to which a buyer was subject when he agreed to buy, there is **no uniquely just**

way of doing this. For instance, should psychological and economic pressure be put on a level with physical pressure?

General rules have to be adapted to special cases, but there is more than one way in which this can be done. It would be unjust to disregard the circumstances of each case, even though we often cannot point to one and only one just way of deciding the case when they are taken into account.

The view that we can sometimes tell what is unjust, but often cannot point in advance to exactly what justice requires in a particular case, seems unsatisfactory. But the just decision is often, I believe, the decision that an impartial and well-informed person will arrive at after carefully considering the facts and the arguments on both sides. Not all judges and lawyers have these qualities but, if they do, the society they serve comes as close to justice as it is possible to get.

That is why I said earlier that justice is **partly objective**. The other part, the **subjective** part, consists in entrusting decisions about how laws should be applied to fair-minded and well-informed people.

11

Does law matter?

Does law really matter? Obviously I think that it does. But can I justify that belief? Or could there be a society, as some Marxists have been inclined to think, so harmonious that it did not need the state and did not need law? Would a classless society, or a society of very high-minded and caring people, need law?

It seems to me that it would. It would be a much better society with law than without it. A classless society will have some selfish people in it. High-minded people differ in their moral outlook and they, like the rest of us, need guidance about how to behave. They may not be inclined to steal, but they need to be informed about what counts as property. They may be committed to avoiding pollution but someone has to decide what the best way of combating it is and to coordinate people's efforts to do so. There has to be authority, and hence law.

The alternative to regulating a society by laws is to regulate it by social pressure or deference — for example deference to a charismatic leader. History seems to show that a society in which deviant behaviour is kept in check in these ways is an unhappy one. We need some protection against social pressures, even those of our family and friends, if we are to flourish. And even the most gifted and well-intentioned leader succumbs in the course of time to the temptations of power if there are no checks on his use of it. This is not to decry social pressure or charisma, but to make the point that they need law to keep them within bounds and check excesses.

The need for law is a need for guidance as to what do, for guarantees that the private arrangements people make will be upheld, and for checks on the abuse of power by rulers. A well-designed legal system therefore consists partly of orders backed by threats of force. These spell out in detail some of the demands of morality and in particular of justice. It also consists of promises that people's rights will be respected, along with guarantees of a remedy if they are not. And it puts some limits on the powers of government.

Because a good legal system has to keep a number of balls in the air at the same time, it is wrong to think of law as **essentially** a system of threats backed by force; or essentially a way of giving effect to morality; or essentially a way of giving effect to people's rights.

All these approaches mistake the part for the whole. The merit of a good legal system is that it strikes a balance between threats and promises. It also strikes a balance between those aspects of morality that the state must enforce and those that can be left to private conscience. It has to compromise between different values, so as to allow people with differing moral, political and social priorities to live together peacefully and securely. This pursuit of balance is in my opinion the essential mark of good law.

Of course there have been and will be bad legal systems. But we are better off with a system that has some bad laws, which we are morally entitled to disobey, than with a society (even a small group) run on social pressure or charisma alone. And it is worth noting that in the most vicious tyrannies, like the Nazi regime, the worst atrocities are usually not based on any law. A cruel ruler is often so ashamed of what he is doing that he does not dare to make a law about it. No law authorized the Holocaust.

Glossary

administrative law	deals with decisions by ministers, public bodies and civil servants and how they can be challenged
arbitration	having a dispute decided not by a judge but by one or more people chosen by the parties
barrister	an advocate in the higher courts in common law countries
bill of rights	a law listing rights of which citizens cannot be deprived so long as the law remains in force
canon law	the law of the western church
case-law	law made by judges in deciding disputes
cause	what produces a given effect
civil law	(a) the law of most European and other non-English-speaking countries, influenced historically by Roman law (b) private law
civil procedure	rules about the steps to be taken in private lawsuits
code	a statute that sets out all the main rules of law on a particular subject
common law	the law of England and most English-speaking countries
contract	a binding agreement between individual people or bodies or between an individual and a state
constitutional law	allots the powers of government to the executive, the legislature, the courts and other bodies
convention	a practice in political life that is treated as binding though not laid down in any law
court	one or more judges with jurisdiction to hear and decide a dispute

criminal procedure	legal rules about the steps to be taken when someone is suspected of or charged with a crime
crime	a wrong that the state is concerned to prevent and punish
damages	compensation for a tort or for breaking a contract
deed	a written document signed by a person making a legally binding promise and witnessed
defendant	the person against whom a lawsuit is brought
delict	the word used for a tort in civil law countries
determinism	the theory that we can never do anything except what we actually do
equity	a body of judge-made law based on the power of a court to make exceptions in order to avoid hardship in particular cases
executive	the government that enforces the laws of a state and itself makes (mostly) minor laws
fault	intending harm or negligently failing to avoid it
federal state	one in which the powers of government are divided between a central government and regional governments
habeas corpus	an order to bring someone who is detained before a court so that he will be released if there is no good reason for detaining him
homicide	killing someone unlawfully
interpretation	deciding what a law means in order to apply it to a particular case
intestate	dying without making a will
invalid	not legally binding
judicial review	the right of judges to decide whether the executive (or in some countries the legislature) has acted legally
jurisdiction	the right of a court to hear and decide a case
jury	a group of ordinary citizens who hear evidence, decide the facts of a case and give a verdict
legislature	the body or bodies that make and repeal laws
manslaughter	killing by recklessness or gross negligence

negligence	not taking enough care or showing enough skill in the circumstances
notary	a lawyer who specializes in drawing up legal documents
objective (as opposed to **subjective**)	
	independent of anyone's individual point of view
obligation	a duty that one is bound to perform or suffer for not performing
owner	the person who has the long-term right to possess something
party	(a) a person who makes an agreement (b) the plaintiff or defendant in a lawsuit
plaintiff	the person who brings a lawsuit
possession	control of property recognized by the law
precedent	a judicial decision that may or must be followed in similar cases
presumption of innocence	
	the rule that the state must prove that the person charged has committed the crime
private law	the law about disputes between individuals (also called civil law)
(legal) procedure	steps that have to be taken to achieve a certain legal result
property	(a) something over which a person can have a right that excludes others (b) the connection between an owner and the thing he owns
public law	constitutional and administrative law
regulation	(a) a legal rule made by the executive (b) a rule creating a minor crime
remedies	steps that a person who has suffered a legal wrong can take
repeal	revoke a law
rescind	undo a contract or other arrangement
restitution	restoring a benefit to the person from whom one got it
right	a person's interest that must be respected by other people and by the state
sanction	something unpleasant which can be imposed on a person or state that does wrong

separation of powers	the principle that the functions of the legislature, the executive government and the judges are distinct and should be entrusted to different people
sovereign	(a) a state that is independent in international law (b) a legislature that can make any law it chooses
specific performance	an order to carry out a promise as agreed
state	(a) a country that is independent in international law (b) in some federations the regions (e.g. California, New South Wales) are called 'states'
statute	a law made by a legislature
strict liability	being liable to punishment or to pay compensation even if not personally at fault
subjective (as opposed to **objective**)	
	depending on a particular person's make-up, opinion etc.
(legal) **system**	the laws of a particular state or country or of the international community
testator	a person who makes a will stating what is to happen to his property when he dies
tort	a wrong for which the person harmed can claim compensation. Called a delict in civil law countries
treaty	a binding agreement between states
valid	legally binding